GREAT WEEK AND PASCHA
IN THE GREEK ORTHODOX CHURCH

GREAT WEEK AND PASCHA

IN THE

GREEK ORTHODOX CHURCH

by

Alkiviadis C. Calivas

HOLY CROSS ORTHODOX PRESS

Brookline, Massachusetts

Fifth Printing, 2004

© Copyright 1992 Holy Cross Orthodox Press
Published by Holy Cross Orthodox Press
50 Goddard Avenue
Brookline, Massachusetts 02445

ISBN 0-917651-97-9

LIBRARY OF CONGRESS CATALOGING–IN–PUBLICATION DATA

Calivas, Alkiviadis C.
Great Week and Pascha in the Greek Orthodox Church/ by
Alkiviadis C. Calivas
     p.   cm.
Includes bibliographical references.
ISBN 0-917651-97-9 (pbk. : alk. paper)
1. Holy Week. 2. Easter. 3. Orthodox Eastern Church—
Liturgy. 4. Greek Orthodox Archdiocese of North and
South America—Liturgy. I. Title
BX376.35.H64C35   1992   92-11382
264'.019 — dc20   CIP

CONTENTS

To the memory of my revered spiritual father
Gerasimos, Bishop of Abydos.

To my students
whose faith commitment, devotion to the Church,
varied gifts and talents, and eagerness to learn
and serve never cease to amaze me.

To my grandchildren
Anastasia and Zachary Newkirk
Alexis, Nicole and Christopher Chininis
and
Andrew, Matthew and Damon Calivas.

For the joy they bring to my heart.

ACKNOWLEDGMENTS

During the last twelve years I have had the special privilege to celebrate the divine services of Great Week and Pascha at the Holy Cross Chapel in the company of respected hierarchs, gifted chanters, devout worshipers, and most especially the students of each entering class of Holy Cross Greek Orthodox School of Theology.

In addition to the divine services, I shared with these students a special seminar, held daily, at which we discussed together the theological, liturgical, and pastoral dimensions of the solemnities of Great Week. These seminars afforded me the opportunity to delve further into the liturgical data and to deepen and broaden my own understanding and appreciation of the Paschal mystery as it is observed and celebrated by our Orthodox Church. This book represents basically the content of the Holy Week Seminar lectures which I shared over the years with the students. At their prompting and urging, I have reworked the class notes and offer them through this book to the general readership as an introduction to Great Week and Pascha.

The book is intended primarily to help the seminarian better understand and more fully appreciate the liturgical wealth and the profound theological and spiritual riches contained in the divine services of Great Week and Pascha. It is dedicated to them in the hope that it will aid them to become knowledgeable and inspired celebrants of the divine mysteries and sacred services of the Church.

The book is offered as well to my fellow priests, as a token of my esteem, affection and appreciation for their faithful pastoral ministry. Among them I acknowledge with special affection my classmates, Holy Cross Class of 1956.

This book would not have been possible except for the unfailing support of family and friends. I wish to express my deep gratitude to all who encouraged me in this endeavor.

It is fitting that I acknowledge the strong support I received from Bishop Methodios, President of Hellenic College and Holy Cross, who unhesitatingly authorized the publication of the manuscript.

Many thanks go to several colleagues on the faculty of Holy Cross, and especially to Father Theodore Stylianopoulos and Father Emmanuel Clapsis, who helped me with the preparation of sections of the manuscript.

I am especially grateful to two distinguished scholars, Metropolitan Demetrios of Vresthena and Father Gabriel Bertoniere, for reviewing the entire manuscript and offering me critical comments and invaluable suggestions.

I am thankful to my venerable spiritual father, Bishop Gerasimos of Abydos, for his paternal interest and encouragement, and especially for his many helpful insights. I owe a debt of gratitude to my beloved student Theodore J. Barbas, for his persistent encouragment and invaluable assistance in the preparation of the manuscript. I thank also my secretary, Mrs. Fotene Diamond Zimmerman and Dr. Robert Newman for their contributions. I am grateful, as well, to Father N. Michael Vaporis, Director of the Holy Cross Orthodox Press, and his staff, especially Stelyio Muksuris, for their technical assistance and for guiding this book to print.

I cannot close these acknowledgments without expressing my debt, appreciation, and deep filial agape and respect to His Eminence Archbishop Iakovos. This book would not have been brought to fruition without his encouragement, support, and approval. I am especially honored that he accepted to write the Foreword.

Brookline, Massachusetts
December 12, 1991
The Feast of Saint Spyridon

FOREWORD

It is with great excitement that I present to you this erudite study *Great Week and Pascha in the Greek Orthodox Church*, authored by the distinguished Dean of our Holy Cross School of Theology, the Rev. Alkiviadis Calivas. A noted scholar in the area of Liturgics, Fr. Calivas gives to the reader a day-by-day overview of the services leading up to and culminating in the "Feast of Feasts," Pascha. He offers insight into the liturgical evolution of this week as well as an essential understanding of its spiritual impact and meaning in the life of clergy and laity alike.

For this reason, I recommend it to all those who seek to heighten their appreciation of this sacred period of the Church calendar and to everyone who seeks "to grow in the grace and knowledge of our Lord and Savior Jesus Christ." You will derive both knowledge and edification as well as inspiration and deeper understanding of the sacred and mystical beauty of the Holy and Great Week as it is celebrated in our Greek Orthodox Church.

I commend Fr. Calivas for his efforts and trust that through this publication the faithful will gain a new and fuller perception of the holiness and greatness of our Holy Week and Pascha.

With paternal blessings,

+ Archbishop Iakovos

+ I A K O V O S
Archbishop of the Greek Orthodox
Church of North and South America

Introduction

THE ORIGINS OF PASCHA AND GREAT WEEK

In worship we encounter the living God. Through worship God makes Himself present and active in our time, drawing the particles and moments of our life into the realm of redemption. He bestows upon us the Holy Spirit, who makes real the promise of Jesus to be in the midst of those gathered in His name (Mt 18.20). In our ecclesial assemblies, therefore, we do more than remember past events and recall future promises. We experience the risen Christ, who is "clothed with his past and future acts," as someone has noted. Thus, all that is past and all that is future are made present in the course of our liturgical celebrations.

Pascha,[1] which commemorates the resurrection of our Lord and Savior Jesus Christ, is the oldest, most venerable and pre-eminent feast of the Church. It is the great Christian festival, the very center and heart of the liturgical year.

Jesus' passion, death and resurrection constitute the essence of His redemptive work. The narrative of these salvific actions of the Incarnate Son of God formed the oldest part of the Gospel tradition.[2] The solemn celebrations of Great Week and Pascha are centered upon these events. The divine services of the Week, crafted long ago in continuity with the experience, tradition and faith of the first Christians, help us penetrate and celebrate the mystery of our salvation.

The prototype of Pascha is the Jewish Passover, the festival of Israel's deliverance from bondage. Like the Old Testament Passover, Pascha is a festival of deliverance. But its nature is wholly other and unique, of which the Passover is only a prefigurement. Pascha involves the ultimate redemption, i.e., the deliverance and liberation of all humanity from the malignant power of Satan and death, through the death and resurrection of Christ. Pascha is the feast of universal redemption. Our earliest sources for the annual celebration of the Christian Pascha come to us from the second century.[3] The feast, however, must have originated in the apostolic period. It would be difficult, if not impossible, to imagine otherwise. The first Christians were Jews and obviously con-

1

scious of the Jewish festal calendar. They scarcely could have forgotten that the remarkable and compelling events of Christ's death, burial and resurrection had occured at a time in which the annual Passover was being observed. These Christians could not have failed to project the events of the passion and the resurrection of Christ on the Jewish festal calendar, nor would they have failed to connect and impose their faith on the annual observance of the Jewish Passover.[4] St. Paul seems to indicate as much when writing to the Corinthians, "purge out the old leaven, that you may be a new lump, since you truly are unleavened. For indeed Christ, our Passover, was sacrificed for us. Therefore let us keep the feast, not with old leaven, nor with the leaven of malice and wickedness, but with the unleavened bread of sincerity and truth" (1 Cor 5.7-8).[5]

The early Church rejoiced in the event of the Resurrection. The new and principal day of worship of the Christians was the first day of the Jewish week, i.e., the day in which the Lord was raised from the dead. They assembled on that day[6] to celebrate the Eucharist, through which they proclaimed the Lord's death and confessed his resurrection.[7] Eventually they gave this day a Christian name, the Day of the Lord, Κυριακὴ Ἡμέρα (Rev 1.10). It would be hard to imagine that the Christians of the first century would not have projected and connected in some new and significant way their weekly celebration of the sacred events of Christ's death and resurrection on the annual observance of the Passover.

Another point of interest in this connection is the emergence of the paschal fast and vigil. According to the earliest documents, Pascha is described as a nocturnal celebration with a long vigil, that was preceded by a fast.[8] This suggests a connection with the Jewish rites of the Passover, even though there is a distinct difference of faith and rite between the Jewish and Christian observance. One such difference centers on the time of the celebration. The Jewish rite was an evening meal that ended at midnight while the Christian festival consisted of a long vigil that ended in the early dawn. It may well be that this delay was intentional, in order to distinguish the Christian night from the Jewish. Furthermore, the delay symbolized the fulfillment of the Passover by Christ, and thus signaled the transition from the old to the new Pascha. It has been suggested that this particular feature of the Paschal night prompted the persistent demand, which we encounter early on, that the Christian Pascha must come after the Jewish Passover.[9]

According to the chronology of the Gospel of John, the Lord was crucified and buried on the day before the Passover and rose the day after.[10] In the year we have come to number 33 A.D., the Passover fell on a Saturday. The crucifixion, therefore, occurred on Friday, while the resurrection happened early Sunday morning.[11] Eventually, the celebration of Pascha in the early Church would be predicated upon this chronology.

In the beginning, the Christian Pascha was the occasion for the remembrance of the entire work of redemption, with a special reference to the Cross and the Resurrection. By the second century the churches of Asia Minor had come to observe Pascha on the 14 of Nisan, the day on which the Lord was crucified, while all the other churches observed Pascha on the Sunday after the 14 of Nisan, emphasizing the resurrection.[12] These two ways of computing the date of Pascha gave rise to the Paschal controversies of the second century. At the beginning of the third century, these disputes were settled in favor of the Sunday observance of Pascha. However, difficulties with inadequate calendars continued to plague the local churches, until the issue was finally resolved by the First Ecumenical Synod of Nicea in 325 A.D. The Fathers of the Synod decreed that henceforth Pascha was to be celebrated on the first Sunday, after the first full moon of the spring equinox. The Synod, also, determined that the date would be calculated in accordance with the Alexandrian calendar. The Orthodox Church continues to maintain this order.[13]

In the early Church, according to local custom, the celebration of Pascha was preceded by a one or two day fast. In a letter written to Pope Victor regarding the Paschal disputes, St. Irenaios (+ ca. 200) makes mention of the fasting practices that were being observed in his time by various local churches. He wrote, "for the controversy is not only concerning the day, but also concerning the very manner of the fast. For some think that they should fast one day, others two, yet others more; some moreover, count their day as consisting of forty hours day and night. And this variety in its observance has not originated in our time; but long before in that of our ancestors.''[14]

It is clear from this testimony that fasting had become an integral element of the Paschal observance from the apostolic period. It probably came about as a result of the words of the Lord, ''can the wedding guests mourn as long as the bridegroom is with them? The days will come, when the bridegroom is taken away from them, and then they will fast'' (Mt 9.15). The Paschal fast, mournful in nature, came to honor the Bridegroom of the Church, who was taken away, crucified, and buried.

The original one or two day fast was expanded by many local churches to include the whole week before Pascha.[15] This process began in the third century. During the course of the fourth century the week long fast had become a universal practice, and the week itself came to be known as ''Holy and Great'' ('Αγία καὶ Μεγάλη 'Εβδομάς'').

The one week fast was increased still further by another development: the formation of the forty day period of the Great Fast or Lent ('Αγία καὶ Μεγάλη Τεσσαρακοστή).[16] Lent represents the maximum expansion of the paschal fast. Though linked to the six day fast of the Great Week, the Lenten fast is separate and distinct from it.[17]

The celebrations of the Great Week developed gradually and in stages. The chronology of the sacred events of the serial aspects of the passion and the resurrection, as recorded in the Gospel of John, would effect the development of the last three days of the Week (Thursday, Friday and Saturday); while the sayings of the Lord and the events in His life immediately preceding the passion, as recorded in the Synoptic Gospels, would effect the development of the first three days of the Week (Monday, Tuesday and Wednesday). In a subsequent development, the chronology of events pertaining to the raising of Lazaros and the triumphant entry of Jesus into Jerusalem, according to the Gospel of John, would bring about the configuration of a two day festival (the

Saturday of Lazaros and the Sunday of Palms) immediately preceding the Great Week. These two festal days anticipate the joy and the victory of the resurrection, and bridge the Great Fast with the Great Week.

The single liturgical event commemorating Christ's death and resurrection expanded very early "as a result of a more historically oriented approach and a more representational type of presentation" of the Paschal mystery.[18] Each aspect of the mystery was broken down, emphasized ritually, and assigned to the day of the week in which it had occurred.

Thus Great Week was born. The crucifixion, burial and resurrection of Christ, together with the event of the Mystical Supper, constituted the very heart and center of the Great Week. The solemn celebration of these events began on Thursday evening and ended on the early dawn of Sunday. During the course of the fourth century a process was set in motion by which the solemnities of the Week would be further enhanced and elaborated.

THE TEXT

An Historical Overview

The divine services of Great Week are an expanded version of the series of services of the daily cycle of worship.[19] As we shall see below, the services from Great Monday to Great Thursday are ordered in accordance with the Lenten form of the weekday services. From Great Friday to Pascha they are structured basically according to the festal form of these services.

The services of the daily cycle contain both fixed and variable elements. The fixed elements of the services are contained in the liturgical book called the Horologion — Ὡρολόγιον; while, in the case of Great Week and Pascha, the variable festal elements are contained in the Triodion — Τριῴδιον and Pentecostarion — Πεντηκοστάριον, respectively. The prayers, petitions and litanies said by the priest and deacon are contained in the Hieratikon — Ἱερατικόν.[20] I mention here briefly, that at the turn of this century both the fixed and variable elements of the services of Great Week, as well as the priestly prayers and petitions were gathered together in one volume, under the title "The Holy and Great Week." But, more will be said about this below.

The variable elements of the divine services of Great Week and Pascha, consist chiefly of a substantial body of hymns and a group of selected readings from the Scriptures. This material is found in the Triodion and Pentecostarion. The Triodion[21] is the liturgical book of the Pre-Lenten and Lenten seasons (Great Fast), as well as Great Week; while the Pentecostarion[22] is the liturgical book of the Paschal season. Together they contain the services of the movable cycle of feasts, which is determined and regulated by the date of Pascha, which changes from year to year. The movable cycle of feasts, with its manifold celebrations of sacred memories and events, covers a period of eighteen weeks and creates a rich and varied landscape in the liturgical year.

At one time these two books constituted a single volume divided into two sections. The first, which is the present Triodion, was known as the Penitential Triodion — Κατανυκτικὸν Τριῴδιον.[23] The second was called the Joyful Triodion or Χαρμόσυνον Τριῴδιον. At one point in the history of their respective development the two sections were separated to form two distinct liturgical books.

The decision to create two separate volumes out of one was of little consequence. However, the point chosen to part the texts in the sequence of the services was significant. The decision to conclude the services of the Triodion with the Paschal Vespers and Liturgy, and to begin the Pentecostarion with the Orthros of Pascha dramatically altered the unity of the Paschal vigil.[24] We shall say more about this below.

The Triodion in its present form was first published in Venice in 1522 while the Pentecostarion was first published in 1568. Much of the material contained in the Triodion and Pentecostarion was composed, compiled and arranged by the monks of the Monastery of Studios in Constantinople during the course of the eighth and ninth centuries. Considerable additional materials, however, were introduced and incorporated into the texts in subsequent centuries, both for the older established feasts as well as for the new and emerging ones.[25] The process of development continued through to the fifteenth-sixteenth centuries. By then, the texts of the divine services had become more or less settled. The same, however, cannot be said about the manner of celebration or ritual action, nor about the order and arrangement of the services. All of these, one could say, continue to be in a state of development.

Characteristically, in our liturgical texts many hymns and prayers do not bear the names of their authors. However, we do know a good number of them.

Many of the hymnographers, whose works are contained in the Triodion, before and after its formative period, came from places other than Constantinople, such as Palestine, Syria, Asia Minor, Greece and Southern Italy. Among these, the most prominent came from the Lavra of St. Savas in Jerusalem.

The hymns of Great Week and Pascha were written by some of the most excellent hymnographers of the Church. Among those whom we can identify we count: Romanos the Melodist (ca. +560); Kosmas the Melodist, Bishop of Maiouma (ca. +750); John of Damascus (ca. +749); Andrew of Crete (ca. +720); Leo the Emperor (ca. +912); and Kassiane (ninth century); and others such as Methodios the Patriarch, Byzantios, Theophanes, Sergios the Logothete, Symeon, George the Akropolites, and Mark the Bishop. Others remain anonymous.

The hymns of Great Week and Pascha are probably the finest example of Orthodox hymnography, which in its totality, according to many, is among the very finest, if not the finest expression of Christian poetry.[26]

The hymns of the divine services we are considering are richly ladened with theology and are replete with biblical language and imagery. They are superbly didactic and inspirational. They reach and touch all aspects of human experience at the deepest level. When properly executed, the nuances of the hymnography are especially enhanced by the traditional chant of the Church. It could be said of these hymns that they are a string of sermonettes in song, especially rich, inspiring and powerful both for their poetic beauty and melodic synthesis, as well as for their theological content and deep spirituality.

We experience worship essentially as a confession of faith. Therefore, the hymns and prayers of the divine services are more doctrinal than lyrical in nature. Thus, the service books of the

Church are counted among the "symbolic books," and count as a source for doctrinal teachings.

The Liturgical Text According to Present Usage

The liturgical books presently used by the Orthodox Church have either originated in the monasteries or have been greatly influenced by monastic practices.

The Typikon of St. Savas

The services of the daily cycle of worship as we know them today, reflect monastic usages and traditions; especially of the two monastic centers that produced and developed them, i.e., the Holy Lavra of St. Savas of Jerusalem and the Monastery of Studios in Constantinople.

The monastic liturgical tradition of the Orthodox East has come down to us through the "Typikon of the Church Service of the Holy Lavra at Jerusalem of our God-bearing Father St. Savas," popularly known as "The Typikon of St. Savas."[27] As the title indicates, this Typikon originated at the Lavra founded by St. Savas (+532) at Jerusalem in the year 484.[28] In the initial stages of its development, the Typikon was influenced by practices and customs of the early monastic communities in Egypt, Palestine and Asia Minor, as well as the Cathedral Office of Jerusalem, which had become a center of pilgrimage. During the seventh and eighth centuries the Typikon of St. Savas was revised and greatly enriched by the massive infusion of ecclesiastical poetry. In the course of the eighth century as a result of the iconoclastic controversy, the Palestinian monastic Typikon came to the monasteries of Constantinople, and especially to the Monastery of Studios. Due to the work of its hegoumenos St. Theodore (+826), this monastery had become the center of monastic revival and reform in the Imperial City. At Studios the Palestinian Typikon underwent a new synthesis. It was embellished further with new poetry and with elements of the Cathedral Office of Constantinople. The Studite rite spread to other monastic communities as well.[29]

In a subsequent development, the Studite synthesis was reworked and further modified by Palestinian monks during the course of the eleventh century. In the process a new, revised Typikon of St. Savas was produced and established. This new revised monastic Typikon soon gained in popularity and use. At the beginning of the thirteenth century it began to replace both the Cathedral Office as well as the Studite synthesis at Constantinople. By the fifteenth century these usages had become defunct. The new, revised Typikon of St. Savas prevailed throughout the Orthodox world, until the nineteenth century.[30] The position of the new Sabaite Typikon was especially solidified in the sixteenth century by virtue of its publication in 1545, thus becoming the earliest of the printed typika.

These revisions together with the infusion of new poetry composed by Sabaite and Studite monks and others, resulted in the formation of the Horologion and the liturgical books we know as the Octoechos, Triodion, Pentecostarion, and Menaia.

The Cathedral or Sung Office

The Cathedral Office or Rite represents the type of services and liturgical traditions which from ancient times were practiced in the parochial or secular churches. These rites are called Cathedral, because the bishop's church was considered the center of all liturgical life. Consequently, the liturgical practices of the cathedral churches permeated the parishes.

In time, the Cathedral of Hagia Sophia at Constantinople would emerge as the single most significant Church edifice in the East. As Robert Taft has noted, ". . . in no liturgical tradition has one edifice played such a decisive role as Justinian's Hagia Sophia . . . where the Byzantine rite was molded and celebrated, and where the vision of its meaning, enacted elsewhere on a smaller stage, was determined and kept alive."[31]

The Cathedral Office at Constantinople, known also as the Sung or Secular Service ('Ασματικὴ ἢ Κοσμικὴ 'Ακολουθία), was regulated by the Typikon of the Great Church.[32] It was called by that name, because Hagia Sophia itself was known as the Great Church (Μεγάλη 'Εκκλησία).

The Cathedral Office had four services for the daily cycle: Vespers, Pannychis, Orthros and Trithekte. The structure, order and number of services differed from the Monastic Office. While

elaborate and imposing, the Cathedral Office lacked the large body
of hymnody contained in the revised Monastic Office. By com-
parison it had become the more staid of the two. For this and
other reasons, it finally fell into disuse. However, as we have noted
above, various elements of the Cathedral Office had already passed
into the monastic Typikon. From the fifteenth century until 1838
all Orthodox Churches, whether parish or monastic, followed the
same basic Typikon of St. Savas.

Typikon of the Great Church of Christ

By the beginning of the nineteenth century it had become obvious that the monastic typikon could not be sustained in parish
usage. Already, numerous abbreviations and omissions were taking
place. The Ecumenical Patriarchate, in an effort to forestall further arbitrary changes as well as to sanction existing practices
and traditions, took an enormous first step towards revising the
typikon and accommodating it to parish usage. In 1838 it authorized the publication of the *The Ecclesiastical Typikon according
to the Style of the Great Church of Christ — Τυπικὸν Ἐκκλησι-
αστικὸν κατὰ τὸ ὕφος τῆς τοῦ Χριστοῦ Μεγάλης Ἐκκλησίας*, prepared by the Protopsaltis, Konstantinos. This typikon was clearly
intended for parish use.

Subsequently, in order to correct the mistakes of Konstantinos,
as well as to incorporate further revisions, the Ecumenical Patriarchate established two committees, one under Patriarch Joachim
III (1878-84) and another under Patriarch Dionysios V (1887-1891),
to study the issue of the Typikon and to make further recommen-
dations. As a result of these efforts, the Patriarchate authorized
in 1888 the publication of a second revised Typikon prepared by
the Protopsaltis, George Violakis, under the title *Typikon of the
Great Church of Christ — Τυπικὸν τῆς τοῦ Χριστοῦ Μεγάλης
Ἐκκλησίας*. Violakis made many changes, including abbreviations
and changes in the order of the services. The new typikon did
not create a body of new material; but it did create a new liturgical
practice, which is essentially a revised and abbreviated monastic
office adapted to parochial usage.[33]

It may be, as it has been suggested,[34] that some of the revisions made by Violakis were ill-advised. Yet, inspite of its short-comings, the effort must be commended as a necessary response of the Church to emerging needs and circumstances.[35]

The new Typikon of Constantinople was adopted gradually by: the churches under the immediate jurisdiction of the Patriarchate; all Greek-speaking churches; and to a varying degree by other churches. The older Typikon of St. Savas continues to be used by most monastic communities, as well as the Churches of Jerusalem and Russia and others.

Liturgical Texts

The decision to develop a new Typikon, in order to regulate liturgical practices in the parishes and to give formal approval to established usages, was not free from difficulties and problems. One such problem was related to the liturgical texts themselves and the need to bring them into conformity with the new regulations. This was a formidable as well as a sensitive task. Nevertheless, the need was real and obvious. A process, though gradual and slow, was set in motion to accomplish the job. That process is still evolving.

To avert unnecessary tensions, one solution to the problem was to continue publishing the books related to the daily office (i.e. the Octoechos, Triodion, Pentekostarion and Horologion), in the traditional manner. This avoided the necessity to alter and or abbreviate the venerable texts. The priestly books, however, and the guides for chanters and readers reflected the order of the new Typikon. The burden was placed on the clergy and the chanters to wade through the materials and decipher the order. While this arrangement for the most part prevails to the present day, it had become obvious that it could not apply to the celebration of Great Week without severe difficulties.

Thus, in 1906 the Ecumenical Patriarchate approved the publication of a single volume containing the services of Great Week and Pascha, under the title *The Holy and Great Week* — Ἡ Ἁγία καὶ Μεγάλη Ἑβδομάς. Besides the material from the Triodion and Pentecostarion, the volume contained priestly prayers and petitions, the designated pericope of the Scriptures and other useful items. The order of the divine services was in accordance with rubrics of the new Typikon of Constantinople.

This text spread and prevailed throughout the Greek-speaking Orthodox Churches. For the purposes of our study we shall refer to it as the Patriarchal Text. The order of the divine services described below is based on this text.

The Patriarchal Text was compiled and edited by Nikodemos P. G. Neokles,[36] a cleric of the Ecumenical Patriarchate. This volume, however, was not unique. A similar work containing the divine services of Lent and Great Week was published a decade earlier by another cleric, Emmanuel Liodopoulos.[37]

The Patriarchal Text of the Great Week was republished by the Apostolike Diakonia of the Church of Greece in 1953.[38] This and subsequent editions of "The Holy and Great Week" of the Apostolike Diakonia found wide, if not universal, use among the Greek Orthodox parishes in the United States.

However, the demand for a bilingual text for use by the faithful of the Greek Orthodox Archdiocese of North and South America was becoming more apparent. To meet this need Archbishop Michael in 1952 commissioned the Press of the Holy Cross Greek Orthodox School of Theology to reprint the Greek-English text of *The Services for Holy Week and Easter Sunday From the Triodion and Pentecostarion*, printed by Williams and Norgate of London in 1915. This edition was soon exhausted.

To fill this void, Father George Papadeas, a priest of the Greek Orthodox Archdiocese, compiled, edited and published in 1963 a new bilingual volume of the services of Great Week and Pascha. This book has been reprinted several times and has enjoyed considerable popularity. Because of this, it could be said that in some respects, it has determined the manner by which the divine services are celebrated and observed in many parishes of the Greek Orthodox Archdiocese.

These English translations, together with others, such as the *Book of Divine Prayers and Services*, compiled and arranged by Father Seraphim Nassar (published in 1938) and the *Service Book of the Holy Orthodox-Catholic Apostolic Church* compiled, translated and arranged by Isabel Florence Hapgood (1906 and

1922) found wide appeal and use among Orthodox peoples in the Americas.[39]

Immensely important contributions to the study and knowledge of the liturgical tradition and rites of the Orthodox Church have been the publication of *The Festal Menaion* (in 1969, 1977) and The *Lenten Triodion* (in 1978), translated from the original Greek by Mother Mary and Archimandrite (now Bishop) Kallistos Ware. The excellent translation, as well as the scholarly introductory sections, appendices and notes provide the reader with a wealth of information and a deep appreciation of Orthodox liturgical theology.

Finally, we should note that during the course of Great Week, besides the services of the daily cycle of worship, we celebrate also the following services: the Liturgy of the Pre-Sanctified Gifts, on the first three days;[40] the Vesperal Divine Liturgy of St. Basil on Great Thursday and at the Paschal Vigil;[41] and the Divine Liturgy of St. John Chrysostom after the Paschal Orthros. On Great Wednesday we conduct the Sacrament of Holy Unction,[42] and, in some places, especially in Cathedral Churches, the service of the "Washing of the Feet" on Great Thursday.[43]

THE TRANSPOSITION OF THE SERVICES

Throughout the centuries the faithful have observed Great Week and Pascha with fervor and great solemnity. Twice each day in the morning and in the evening, they would gather in the churches to celebrate the designated service at the appointed times.

However, at some point in history the appointed times of the services began to change. The morning services were moved to the preceding evening and the evening services to the morning. It is not clear when and why these changes began to occur. By the middle of the nineteenth century, if not much sooner, it had become a common practice throughout the Orthodox Church. P. Rombotes in his book Χριστιανικὴ Ἠθικὴ καί Λειτουργικὴ[44] published in Athens in 1869 makes reference to the custom, as does the new Typikon of Constantinople.[45] The reasons for the change appear to be ambiguous. Both Rombotes and the Typikon mention that it was done to accommodate the people.[46] This may

have meant any number of things. For example, the new Typikon
hints at one such possibility. By mentioning the fact that the services were very lengthy, it implies that the transposition occured
in order to address this problem.[47] Another reason for the
change may have come about as a result of some socio-political
factors during the Ottoman rule. For example, a rule regulating
the time for the public assembly of the Christian populace may
have resulted in the shift of the services. Sometimes, an imposed
practice in one generation or period has a way of becoming
permanent.

Perhaps the most plausible reason for the rearrangement of
the divine services is based on late medieval attitudes concerning
the time of the celebration of the Divine Liturgy and the reception of Holy Communion. According to long held popular beliefs,
it was thought that the morning hours of the day were the most
suitable and acceptable for the reception of Holy Communion.
This being the case, it follows that all celebrations of the Divine
Liturgy should be placed in the morning hours, regardless of the
fact that some such celebrations were in fact nocturnal in nature.

An additional factor of considerable importance, which may
also help explain the transfer of the morning services to the
previous evening is the vigil or extended nocturnal service. There
were several different types of vigils in the early and medieval
Church.[48] Their structure, content and length varied according
to purpose and local custom and usage. They were conducted as
late night, all-night or pre-dawn observances. Vigils were held on
the eve of great feasts as a sign of watchfulness and expectation.
We know from several early and medieval documents that the Passion of our Lord was observed liturgically in both Jerusalem and
Constantinople with some type of vigil service.[49] There is sufficient evidence to connect the present Great Friday Orthros with
these earlier vigil services. It is reasonable to assume from this
that the present Orthros was originally observed as a nocturnal
celebration. Thus, as the order and hours of the divine services
of Great Week began to change and shift, this service — and by
extension the other morning services of the Week — was advanced
to earlier evening hours.

Whatever the reasons for the transposition of the services, we have in fact inherited a particularly peculiar tradition, which circumvents both the normal liturgical practice as well as the natural order of things. Beginning with Great Monday and lasting through Great Saturday, the divine services are in an inverted position. Morning services are conducted the evening before and evening services are celebrated in the morning of the same day. Thus, on Palm Sunday evening, we conduct the Orthros of Great Monday and on the morning of Great Monday we celebrate the Vespers with the Pre-Sanctified Liturgy.[50] This pattern places us one half day ahead of the historical events and the natural order.

Of particular interest in this matter, is the order of the divine services for Great Thursday contained in the now defunct Typikon of the Great Church.[51] The services of the Orthros and the Trithekte in this Typikon are assigned to the morning hours, while a series of long services are designated for the evening hours. They are: the Vespers, followed by the Nipter (Washing of the feet), to which the Divine Liturgy of St. Basil is added beginning with the entrance of the Gospel. Before Holy Communion was distributed, the Patriarch also consecrated the Holy Myron. After the Divine Liturgy came the service of the Pannychis. In the Cathedral Office the Pannychis was a type of vigil service. This particular Pannychis on Great Thursday commemorated the passion of the Lord ("Τῇ δὲ αὐτῇ ἑσπέρᾳ εἰς τὴν παννυχίδα τῶν παθῶν τοῦ Κυρίου ἡμῶν Ἰησοῦ Χριστοῦ . . ."). The twelve Gospel pericopes narrating the events of the passion were read at this service. These pericopes are the same as those now read in the present service of the Orthros of Great Friday, which in current practice is conducted on the evening of Great Thursday by anticipation.

From this description we learn at least two things. First, that Great Thursday evening in the late medieval church was supplied heavily with a series of long services. Second, the commemoration of the passion was conducted in the context of a vigil service (the Pannychis) on the night of Great Thursday. Because of the length of these services, I think we can safely assume they lasted well into the night. Can we assume also that Great Thursday evening with its overburdened liturgy became the pivotal day in the process that saw the breakdown of liturgical units and their transposition to earlier hours? The Vesperal Divine Liturgy, for the reasons stated above, may well have been the first to be dislodged from its original moorings, moving steadily forward in the day until it came to be celebrated in the morning hour. Next, the Pannychis or Vigil lost its original meaning and began to gravitate to an earlier hour. As these arrangements gradually evolved, the transposition of the morning services to the preceeding evening became the established practice.

Difficult as it may be, however, I believe that the Church is obliged to press the issue through careful study and find a way to restore the proper liturgical order. She can do no less, if she is to be true to her quest for and commitment to liturgical renewal and reform. St. Symeon of Thessalonike (+ 1429), an inspired student and teacher of liturgy noted in one of his treatises that once the Church has clarified and determined correct liturgical usages, we are obliged to change even those things that have become a practice by default. While we must honor and reverence our liturgical inheritance, we are also obliged to look at it more carefully and to distinguish between Tradition and custom. Here let me stress the point that it is the Church in her collective wisdom that must authenticate the need and procede to the reform of liturgical practice and usage.

THE ETHOS OF GREAT WEEK

The salvific events, which the Church remembers and celebrates in Great Week, are rooted in the inexhaustible mystery of God's ineffable love for the world that culminated in the incarnation, the death and resurrection of His only-begotten Son and our Lord and Savior, Jesus Christ.

The solemnities of Great Week help us to enter and penetrate the depths of this mystery. Each day has a particular theme, focus and story. Each story is linked to the other; and all together, they are bound up in the central event: the Pascha of the cross and the resurrection — the σταυρώσιμον καὶ ἀναστάσιμον Πάσχα. Everything converges on the person of Jesus Christ, who was betrayed, crucified and buried; and who rose on the third day.

These events are the keystones of the structure of Great Week. Through them we embrace the mystery of our salvation. Their radiance helps us to see again more clearly the depth of our sins, both personal and collective. Their power bursts upon us to remind us again of God's immeasurable love, mercy and power. Their truth confronts us again with the most crucial challenge: "to dare to be saints by the power of God . . . To dare to have holy respect and reverence for ourselves, as we are redeemed and sanctified by the blood of Christ . . . To dare to have the courage to grasp the great power that has been given to us, at the same time realizing that this power is always made perfect in infirmity, and that it is not a possession."[52]

Great Week brings us before two realities. On the one hand we are made aware of the dreadful blight of human sin, issuing from the rebellion against God that resides in us and around us; on the other hand, we experience anew the omnipotent, transforming power of God's love and holiness.

From the beginning, Jesus and His gospel were met by a twofold response: some believed and became His disciples; others rejected Him and came to hate him, and to despise and scorn His Gospel.[53] These opposing attitudes towards the person and the message are especially evident in the events of Great Week. As the events unfold, false religiosity is unmasked (Mt 23.2-38); and the hellish bowels of the power of darkness are laid bare (Lk 22.53). Ensconced in the hearts of evil men — demonic, malignant and odious — the darkness seethes with deception, slander, deviousness, greed, cowardice, treachery, betrayal, perfidy, rejection, hatred and aggressive hostility. Evil, in all its absurdity and fury, explodes on the Cross. But it is rendered powerless by the love of God (Lk 23.34). Christ is victor. Death is swallowed up. The tombs are emptied (Mt 27.52-53). Life is liberated. God and not man controls the destiny of the world.

In the course of the events of Great Week we encounter many contrasting figures and faces that call to judgement our own dispositions towards Christ. Great Week is not simply a time to remember; it is a time for repentance, for a greater and deeper conversion of the heart. Two hymns from the Orthros of Great

Tuesday say it best:

> O Bridegroom, surpassing all in beauty, Thou hast called us to the spiritual feast of Thy bridal chamber. Strip from me the disfigurement of sin, through participation in Thy sufferings; clothe me in the glorious robe of Thy beauty, and in Thy compassion make me feast with joy at Thy Kingdom.

> Come ye faithful, and let us serve the Master eagerly, for He gives riches to His servants. Each of us according to the measure that we have received, let us increase the talent of grace. Let one gain wisdom through good deeds; let another celebrate the Liturgy with beauty; let another share his faith by preaching to the uninstructed; let another give his wealth to the poor. So shall we increase what is entrusted to us, and as faithful stewards of His grace we shall be counted worthy of the Master's joy. Bestow this joy upon us, Christ our God, in Thy love for mankind.

In the solemnities of Great Week we experience afresh the embrace of God's love and forgiveness; the gift and promise of eternity and plenitude. Quickened and energized by the experience, we continue by faith to climb the ladder of divine ascent. Certain of His love, we live in the saving tension of joyous-sorrow (χαρμολύπη) until He comes. With a repentant heart we live the joy of hope and the rapture of expectation for things to come (1 Cor 2.9).

CONCLUDING REMARKS

As the order in the liturgical books clearly indicates, the full cycle of the daily services is observed on each day of Great Week at least in principle. In practice, however, parish communal worship is generally centered on the daily Orthros and Vespers and the Divine Liturgies assigned to particular days. In the chapters that follow, I shall endeavor to give a detailed explanation of these divine services as they are currently observed and practiced. Each chapter begins with a brief reflection to help introduce the reader to the inner meaning of the observance. This is followed by some general observations and comments on the liturgical celebration of the day. Then, the order of the divine services of the particular day is presented, together with a description of special rites and an analysis of the rubrics. Finally, the reader will find useful historical, liturgical and bibliographical information in the endnotes.

The descriptions and rubrics of the divine services as we have noted are based chiefly on the book Ἡ Ἁγία καὶ Μεγάλη Ἑβδομάς, authorized by the Ecumenical Patriarchate of Constantinople. For the sake of brevity, further reference to this book will be noted simply as, The Patriarchal Text.

It is hoped that the present study will lead the reader to a deeper appreciation of the spiritual riches contained in the liturgical tradition of the Orthodox Church in general, and in the divine services of Great Week in particular.

Chapter One

The Saturday of Lazaros
and Palm Sunday

COMMENTS ON THE MAIN THEMES

The solemnities of Great Week are preceded by a two-day festival commemorating the resurrection of Lazaros and the triumphant entry of Christ into Jerusalem. These two events punctuate Christ's ministry in a most dramatic way (Jn 11.1-12,19). By causing the final eruption of the unrelenting hostility of His enemies, who had been plotting to kill him, these two events precipitate Christ's death. At the very same time, however, these same events emphasize His divine authority. Through them Christ is revealed as the source of all life and the promised Messiah. For this reason, the interlude which separates Great Week from the Great Fast is Paschal in character. It is the harbinger of Christ's victory over death and of the inrush of His kingdom into the life of the world.

The Saturday of Lazaros is counted among the major feasts of the Church. It is celebrated with great reverence and joy. The event of the raising of Lazaros is recorded in the Gospel of John (11.1-45). The hymnography of the feast interprets the theological significance of the event.[54] Accordingly, the resurrection of Lazaros is viewed as a prophecy in action. It prefigures both the resurrection of Christ,[55] as well as the general resurrection of all the dead in the end times.[56] The hymns of the feast also emphasize the biblical truth that the resurrection as such, is more than an event. It is a person, Christ Himself, who bestows eternal life now upon all who believe in Him, and not at some obscure future time (Jn 11.25-26).[57]

In addition, the resurrection of Lazaros occasioned the disclosure of Christ's two natures, the divine and the human. He manifested His divine power by His foreknowledge of the death of Lazaros and by the final outcome, the miracle of his resurrection. Also, in the course of the dramatic events Jesus displayed

21

deep human emotions. The Gospel records His deep feelings of
love, tenderness, sympathy and compassion, as well as distress and
sadness. The narrative reports that He sighed from the heart and
wept (Jn 11.5, 33, 35, 36, 38).[58]

The Entry into Jerusalem. At the outset of His public ministry
Jesus proclaimed the kingdom of God and announced that the
powers of the age to come were already active in the present age
(Lk 7.18-22). His words and mighty works were performed "to produce repentance as the response to His call, a call to an inward
change of mind and heart which would result in concrete changes
in one's life, a call to follow Him and accept His messianic
destiny."[59]

The triumphant entry of Jesus into Jerusalem is a messianic
event, through which His divine authority was declared.

Palm Sunday summons us to behold our king: the Word of
God made flesh. We are called to behold Him not simply as the
One who came to us once riding on a colt, but as the One who
is always present in His Church, coming ceaselessly to us in power
and glory at every Eucharist, in every prayer and sacrament, and
in every act of love, kindness and mercy. He comes to free us from
all our fears and insecurities, "to take solemn possession of our
soul, and to be enthroned in our heart," as someone has said.
He comes not only to deliver us from our deaths by His death
and resurrection, but also to make us capable of attaining the most
perfect fellowship or union with Him. He is the king, who liberates
us from the darkness of sin and the bondage of death. Palm Sunday summons us to behold our king: the vanquisher of death and
the giver of life.

Palm Sunday summons us to accept both the rule and the
kingdom of God as the goal and content of our Christian life. We
draw our identity from Christ and His kingdom. The kingdom is
Christ — His indescribable power, boundless mercy and incom-
prehensible abundance given freely to man. The kingdom does
not lie at some point or place in the distant future. In the words
of the Scripture, the kingdom of God is not only at hand (Mt 3.2;
4.17), it is within us (Lk 17.21). The kingdom is a present reality
as well as a future realization (Mt 6.10). Theophan the Recluse

wrote the following words about the inward rule of Christ the King:

> The Kingdom of God is within us when God reigns in us, when the soul in its depths confesses God as its Master, and is obedient to Him in all its powers. Then God acts within it as master "both to will and to do of his good pleasure" (Phil 2.13). This reign begins as soon as we resolve to serve God in our Lord Jesus Christ, by the grace of the Holy Spirit. Then the Christian hands over to God his consciousness and freedom, which comprises the essential substance of our human life, and God accepts the sacrifice; and in this way the alliance of man with God and God with man is achieved, and the covenant with God, which was severed by the Fall and continues to be severed by our wilful sins, is re-established.[60]

The kingdom of God is the life of the Holy Trinity in the world.[61] It is the kingdom of holiness, goodness, truth, beauty, love, peace and joy. These qualities are not works of the human spirit. They proceed from the life of God and reveal God. Christ Himself is the kingdom. He is the God-Man, Who brought God down to earth (Jn 1.1,14). "He was in the world, and the world was made through Him, yet the world knew Him not. He came to His own home, and His own people received Him not" (Jn 1.10-11). He was reviled and hated.

Palm Sunday summons us to behold our king — the Suffering Servant. We cannot understand Jesus' kingship apart from the Passion. Filled with infinite love for the Father and the Holy Spirit, and for creation, in His inexpressible humility Jesus accepted the infinite abasement of the cross. He bore our griefs and carried our sorrows; He was wounded for our transgressions and made Himself an offering for sin (Is 53). His glorification which was accomplished by the resurrection and the ascension was achieved through the cross.

In the fleeting moments of exhuberance that marked Jesus' triumphal entry into Jerusalem, the world received its King. The king who was on His way to death. His passion, however, was no morbid desire for martyrdom. Jesus' purpose was to accomplish the mission for which the Father sent Him.[62]

The Son and Word of the Father, like Him without beginning and eternal, has come today to the city of Jerusalem, seated on a dumb beast, on a foal. From fear the cherubim dare not gaze upon Him; yet the children honor Him with palms and branches, and mystically they sing a hymn of praise: "Hosanna in the highest, Hosanna to the Son of David, who has come to save from error all mankind." (A hymn of the *Lite*.)

With our souls cleansed and in spirit carrying branches, with faith let us sing Christ's praises like the children, crying with a loud voice to the Master: Blessed art Thou, O Savior, who hast come into the world to save Adam from the ancient curse; and in Thy love for mankind Thou hast been pleased to become spiritually the new Adam. O Word, who hast ordered all things for our good, glory to Thee. (A Sessional hymn of the *Orthros*)

GENERAL OBSERVATIONS

Vestments — The Saturday of Lazaros and Palm Sunday are joyous festivals. Therefore, the priest wears festive vestments (white, gold, or green). The Holy Table is also adorned with a bright cover.

Palm Branches — The priest should make certain that a sufficient number of palm or some other suitable branches are available for the decoration of the Church and for distribution to the faithful, in accordance with local custom and tradition. It is customary to weave the palm branches into small crosses. The priest may assign this task to a group of parishioners. In some places, the faithful bring their own palms or some similar boughs or branches to the Church.

The priest may choose to have a few acolytes hold palm branches during the two Entrances of the Divine Liturgy. At one time the Church held a procession on Palm Sunday. This tradition has fallen into disuse, except in the churches of the Patriarchate of Antioch. In the Antiochene tradition a procession of the faithful takes place after the Divine Liturgy. An emphasis is placed on the participation of children. The roots of this tradition are to be found in the ancient rites of the Jerusalem Church.[63]

The Blessing and Distribution of the Palms — A basket containing the woven palm crosses is placed on a table in front of the icon of the Lord which is on the Iconostasion.

The prayer for the blessing of the Palms is found in the Ἱερατικὸν or the Εὐχολόγιον. According to the rubrics of the Typikon, this prayer is read at the Orthros just before the Psalms of Praise (Αἶνοι). The palms are then distributed to the faithful.

In many places today, the prayer is said at the conclusion of the Divine Liturgy, before the apolysis. The text of the prayer, however, indicates clearly that it is less a prayer for the blessing of the palms, even though that is its title, and more a blessing upon those, who in imitation of the New Testament event hold palms in their hands as symbols of Christ's victory and as signs of a virtuous Christian life. It appears then, that it would be more correct to have the faithful hold the palms in their hands during the course of the Divine Liturgy when the Church celebrates both the presence and the coming of the Lord in the mystery of the Eucharist. The palms, therefore, should be distributed before the celebration of the Divine Liturgy.

The Icon — On each day we display the appropriate icon of the feast for veneration.[64]

A Folk Tradition — An interesting sidelight is the folk tradition related to the Saturday of Lazaros. In many places groups of children visit neighboring homes to sing the Carols of Lazaros. In return, the people of the house give the children fresh eggs. The children bring the eggs to their homes. On Great Thursday the eggs are boiled in the traditional red dye for the Paschal celebration.

Fasting — By custom and tradition fish as well as oil and wine are permitted on the Saturday of Lazaros and Palm Sunday.

The Apodosis of Palm Sunday — takes place on the same day in the late afternoon with the celebration of the Vesper Service. The service is conducted in accordance with the order in the Triodion. In current usage, however, few parishes conduct this service. It has fallen into disuse.

Removal of the Palms — The palms are removed from the Church at the conclusion of the Vesper Service of the Apodosis of the Feast, or in the late afternoon Palm Sunday.

The Orthros of Great Monday — On Palm Sunday night we observe the beginning of the reversed order of the services, which was noted above. The Orthros of Great Monday is celebrated on Palm Sunday night.

RUBRICS

The Saturday of Lazaros
The Vesper Service is conducted in conjunction with the Pre-Sanctified Liturgy on Friday, the last day of the Great Fast. (If the Pre-Sanctified Liturgy is omitted, the Vesper service is conducted according to the order in the Triodion).
The Orthros is conducted in accordance with the order in the Triodion and the rubrics of the Typikon of the Great Church of Christ.
The Divine Liturgy — We celebrate the Divine Liturgy of St. John Chrysostom.

> *At the Entrance* we sing the Apolytikion of the Feast.
>
> *The Eisodikon* is "Δεῦτε προσκυνήσωμεν . . . ὁ ἀναστὰς ἐκ νεκρῶν . . ." — "Come let us . . . who was resurrected . . ."
>
> *The Kontakion* of the Feast is sung.
>
> *The Trisagion* is replaced by " Ὅσοι εἰς Χριστόν . . ." — "As many as have been baptized . . ."[65]
>
> *The Readings* — We read the Epistle and Gospel of the Feast.
>
> *The "Axion Estin"* is replaced by the Katavasia of the 9th Ode of the Orthros, "Τὴν ἀγνὴν ἐνδόξως τιμήσωμεν. . ." — "With all peoples let us honor . . ."
>
> *The Communion Hymn is* "Ἐκ στόματος νηπίων . . ." — "From the mouths of babes . . ."[66]
>
> *The Eidomen to Phos* is replaced by the Apolytikion "Τὴν κοινὴν ἀνάστασιν . . ." — "Giving us before Your Passion. . ."
>
> *The Apolysis* is "Ὁ ἀναστὰς ἐκ νεκρῶν . . . — He who rose from the dead."

The Sunday of the Palms
    The Great Vesper Service is conducted according to the order in the Triodion and the rubrics of the Typikon. The *apolysis* has

a special prologue: "'Ο ἐπὶ πώλου ὄνου . . . — May He who consented to ride on the foal . . ."

The Orthros is chanted in accordance with the order in the Triodion and the rubrics of the Typicon. It is not a regular Sunday Orthros, but an Orthros of a Dominical Feast (Δεσποτικὴ Ἑορτή). The Morning Gospel of the Feast is read from the Holy Gate.

The Divine Liturgy — We celebrate the Divine Liturgy of St. John Chrysostom.

> The Antiphons are taken from Psalms 114, 115, and 117. The refrain of the 2nd antiphon is "Σῶσον ἡμᾶς . . . ὁ ἐπὶ πώλου ὄνου καθεσθείς . . . — Save us, O Son of God, who sat upon the foal . . ."
>
> *The Entrance* — We sing the Apolytikion of the Feast.
>
> *The Eisodikon* — The "Δεῦτε" is replaced by "Εὐλογημένος ὁ ἐρχόμενος ἐν ὀνόματι Κυρίου. Θεὸς Κύριος καὶ ἐπέφανεν ἡμῖν. Σῶσον ἡμᾶς . . . — Blessed is He that comes in the Name of the Lord . . . Save us, O Son of God, who sat upon the foal . . ."
>
> *The two Apolytikia* of the Feast are sung.[67]
>
> *The Kontakion* of the Feast is sung.
>
> *The usual Trisagion* is sung.
>
> *The Readings* — The assigned Readings of the Epistle and Gospel of the Feast are read (intoned).
>
> *The "Axion Estin"* is replaced by the Katavasia of the 9th Ode: "Θεὸς Κύριος . . . Συστήσασθε ἑορτήν . . ." — "The Lord is God . . ."
>
> *The Communion Hymn* is "Εὐλογημένος ὁ ἐρχόμενος" — Blessed is He . . ." (Ps 117.26).
>
> *The Eidomen to Phos* is replaced by "Τὴν κοινὴν ἀνάστασιν . . . — Giving us before Your Passion . . ."
>
> *The Apolysis* is the same as at the Vesper Service.

Chapter Two

Great Monday, Tuesday, and Wednesday

COMMENTS ON THE MAIN THEMES

The first part of Great Week presents us with an array of themes based chiefly on the last days of Jesus' earthly life. The story of the Passion, as told and recorded by the Evangelists, is preceded by a series of incidents located in Jerusalem and a collection of parables, sayings and discourses centered on Jesus' divine sonship, the kingdom of God, the Parousia, and Jesus' castigation of the hypocrisy and dark motives of the religious leaders. The observances of the first three days of Great Week are rooted in these incidents and sayings. The three days constitute a single liturgical unit. They have the same cycle and system of daily prayer. The Scripture lessons, hymns, commemorations, and ceremonials that make up the festal elements in the respective services of the cycle highlight significant aspects of salvation history, by calling to mind the events that anticipated the Passion and by proclaiming the inevitability and significance of the Parousia.

It is interesting to note that the Orthros of each of these days is called the Service of the Bridegroom (Άκολουθία τοῦ Νυμφίου). The name comes from the central figure in the well-known parable of the ten virgins (Mt 25.1-13). The title Bridegroom suggests the intimacy of love. It is not without significance that the kingdom of God is compared to a bridal feast and a bridal chamber. The Christ of the Passion is the divine Bridegroom of the Church. The imagery connotes the final union of the Lover and the beloved. The title Bridegroom also suggests the Parousia. In the patristic tradition, the aforementioned parable is related to the Second Coming; and is associated with the need for spiritual vigilance and preparedness, by which we are enabled to keep the divine commandments and receive the blessings of the age to come. In addi-

29

tion, knowing something about the structure of the Orthros will help us to further our understanding of the use of the imagery of the Bridegroom. It has been shown that, after the so-called Royal Office and the Hexapsalmos, the first part of the Orthros, as we know and practice it today, is an earlier version of the monastic service of Mesonyktikon (Midnight Service).[68] The Mesonyktikon is centered chiefly on the theme of the Parousia and is linked to the notion of watchfulness. The troparion "Behold the Bridegroom comes in the middle of the night . . .", which is sung at the beginning of the Orthros of Great Monday, Tuesday and Wednesday, relates the worshiping community to that essential expectation: watching and waiting for the Lord, who will come again to judge the living and the dead.

While each day has its own distinct character and its own specific commemoration, they share together several common themes among which are the following.

Conflict, Judgement and Authority

The last days were especially sorrowful and gloomy. The relentless hostility and opposition to Jesus by the religious authorities had reached unparalled proportions. In the midst of this painful conflict Jesus revealed aspects of His divine authority by passing judgement on the evil plots and the false religiosity of His enemies.

The unremitting belligerency of Jesus' adversaries was completely unmasked in the days preceding the crucifixion. The leaders of all the religious parties and factions collaborated and conspired to entrap, humiliate and kill Him. As the snares of His enemies tightened, Jesus openly foretold His death and subsequent glorification. His words were a clear declaration that His death was voluntary and lay within the framework of the divine plan for the salvation of the world. The power being exercised over Him by His enemies was granted and controlled by God (Jn 12.20). The Church commemorates the Passion not as ugly episodes caused by vile and contemptible men, but as the voluntary sacrifice of the Son of God.[69]

Evil in all its absurdity erupted violently on the Cross, in order to destroy and dispose of Jesus and to negate and abolish His message. However, it was evil itself that was rendered fundamentally powerless and ineffectual by the sovereignty of God's love and life. While evil assails the holy ones of God, it cannot destroy them.

The Gospel narrative recounting the events that led to the crucifixion also includes several parables and discourses in which Jesus strongly criticized the religious leaders for their disbelief, obstinacy, authoritarianism, and hypocrisy. The severe critique of the religious classes (Mt 21.28-23,36) is another clear sign of Jesus' authority and excellence. By preserving these sayings of Jesus, the Evangelists declare that Christ is "not only a unique teacher, but also the highest judge. He is one with authority who has the right to judge and condemn"[70] bad and false religious faith and activity.

No disease of the spirit is more insidious, deceptive and destructive than false religiosity, which can be defined succinctly as religious legalism and exhibitionism. Jesus condemned it outrightly. He warned against those whose lives are measured by ceremonials rather than the holiness, mercy and love of God; and those whose evil motivations, intentions and improprieties are cloaked in the respectability of the externals of religious faith and life. False religiosity is a cruel hoax and a betrayal of authentic religious faith. The practitioners of such artificial faith shut the Kingdom of heaven against men, for they neither enter themselves, nor do they allow those who would enter to go in (Mt 23.13).[71]

Mourning and Repentance

The tone of Great Week is clearly one of somberness and sorrowfulness. Even the altar cloths and priestly vestments, according to an old tradition, are black. However, the liturgical assembly is not gathered to mourn a dead hero, but to remember and commemorate an event of cosmic significance: the Son of God experiencing in His humanity every form of suffering at the hands of feeble, misdirected and evil men. We mourn our sinfulness as we stand in contrite silence before the awesome, inscrutable mystery of Christ, the God-man (Θεάνθρωπος), who carries His kenosis to the extreme limits accepting the death of the cross (Phil 2.5-8).

Great Week reveals to us the utter shame of the Fall, the depths of hell, Paradise lost, and the absence of God. And so we mourn! There is no other way to deal with our rebellion and with God's unfathomable humility and condescension except to experience the rending of the heart. It is out of this kind of mourning that true repentance is born, to be experienced as the honest commitment to the life-long process of grasping, accepting and choosing to follow the values fo the Christian life.

The liturgy of the days of the Bridegroom represents the most urgent and emphatic call to such repentance (μετάνοια). The faithful are reminded that no sin is so great as to defy the bounds of divine mercy, for Christ gives everyone the power to slay sin and to share in His victory.[72]

> On the Cross, Jesus has a vision of all those for whom He is dying. He foresees each one of us individually, saving us through His death and by His love . . . He did this to allow God to enter everywhere there is human suffering, even into the abyss of death, accompanying man to the depths of suffering so as to raise him up again and bring him back to life, by lifting him up to heaven and placing him at the right hand of the Father. The Son of God dies as man so that the Son of Man may rise up again as God. The Son of God had to experience the anguish of God's absence so that all men who die might recover the presence of God: this is salvation.[73]

The Parousia

In the days and hours before His passion, Jesus spoke to His disciples about the Parousia, i.e., His second glorious coming. He invites us as well at the beginning of Great Week to approach the mystery and ponder its meaning and significance for our own life and the life of the world.

In the Church we recognize that eternal life has penetrated our finitude. However, we also know that the full realization and revelation of God's kingdom, already begun developing secretly within the world, will occur only at the end of the age, at the Parousia. The Parousia is God's climatic intervention in the history of the cosmos. It is the Last Day, when Christ will come again in all His glory to judge the living and the dead (Mt 16.27; 25.31). Then all things will be made new (Rev 21.5).

While we have only a partial knowledge of the things that pertain to the Last Day, some things are clear and certain.

The end times will appear suddenly and when we least expect them (1 Thes 5.2-3). The exact time of the Parousia is known only to God the Father (Mt 24.36; Acts 1.7). However, according to Jesus' word, this dramatic and decisive event that will mark the sudden end of history, will be preceded by certain signs pointing to the imminent coming of the Bridegroom. It is clear from His words that the Second Coming will not be ushered in by some idyllic interlude, but with unprecedent cosmic calamities, tribulation and distress (Mt 24.1-51; Mk 13.1-37; Lk 21.7-36). The devastation and desolation of the last days has been prefigured mysteriously in the frightening and awesome events that accompanied the crucifixion (Mt 27.27-54).

Regardless of when the Last Day will come, it is always imminent, always spiritually close at hand in the life of every human being.[74] The uncertainties in and the unpredictability of human life allows us to grasp, even vaguely, the imminance of the Parousia. For example, death, the ultimate indignity, abomination and enemy, stalks us from the moment we are born. To obtain the victory of Christ over corruption and death we must remain spiritually watchful; be steadfast in the faith; use our God-given talents wisely; and be constantly aware of the primacy of love in our relationships. The life we live in the flesh is filled with the potential and opportunity to gain heaven or to lose it.

The decisive battle with evil has been waged and won. However, the fullness of that victory will not be realized and manifested until the Parousia. Till then the awkward, senseless and futile efforts of the devil will go on seeking to rob people of their dignity and destiny. Therefore, we are obliged to keep the words of St. Peter the Apostle alive in our memory and operative in our lives. He wrote, "humble yourselves under the mighty hand of God, that in due time He may exalt you. Cast all your anxieties on Him, for He cares about you. Be sober, be watchful. Your adversary the devil prowls around like a roaring lion, seeking some one to devour. Resist him, firm in your faith . . . The God of all grace who has called you to His eternal glory in Christ, will Himself restore, establish and strengthen you" (1 Pt 5.6-10).

The Church is always oriented towards the future, towards the age to come. Thus, the eschaton or Last Day which will usher in God's kingdom in power and glory, forms our point of constant reference both as persons and as community. "The Church does not draw her identity from what she is but from what she will be ... We must think of the eschaton as the beginning of the Church's life, the arche (principle), that brings forth the Church, gives her identity, sustains and inspires her in her existence. The Church exists not because Christ died on the Cross but because He has risen from the dead, which means, because the kingdom has come. The Church reflects the future, the final stage of things, not an historical event of the past."[75] This eschatological vision is a fundamental characteristic of our faith. It fashions the consciousness of Orthodox Christians and inspires and guides the life and activity of the Church.

The Church is primarily a worshiping community constituted by the very presence of God's embracing love. Established by the redeeming action of God, sustained and vivified by the Holy Spirit, the Church at prayer is always being constituted and actualized as the Body of Christ. Permeated by the joyous and overpowering presence of the risen Christ (Mt 28.20), the Church is called both to share in His risen, deified life and to yearn for and expect the coming fullness of the manifestation of His glory and power (2 Pt 3.12). The future age — God's kingdom — is known and experienced by the faithful both as gift and as promise, i.e., as something given and at the same time as something anticipated.

Through worship in general and the sacraments in particular we experience a personal relationship with God, who infuses His life into us. We experience His uncreated energies touching, healing, restoring, purifying, illumining, sanctifying and glorifying both human life and the cosmos. We participate in the saving acts of Christ's life, in order to be continuously renewed. We experience continually the presence of the Holy Spirit dwelling and active within us, leading us to and bestowing upon us the resurrectional life.

Our preparation for the Kingdom has already begun with our baptism and chrismation. It is sustained and advanced through the Eucharist. The sacraments give us powers by which we draw near to Christ and to His kingdom. These powers are dynamic and are meant to be developed by us. Thus, our preparation for the kingdom is a movement that involves progress, both as a return as well as an advance into God.[76] The progress begins with man's return from estrangement to his own authenticity. Fundamentally, this means a return to Christ, the archetype and model of man. At the very same time this return is also a progress forward into God. "Return is simultaneously also progress forward and progress forward is return. It is a return of human nature to itself, and a progress forward into itself, but at the same time it is a return to and a progress forward into God and Christ, for no development of human nature is possible except in God and Christ . . . The new or future age develops by promoting the dissolution or transformation of the present age."[77]

The age to come will not grow out of some biological or historical evolutionary process, nor will it be simply the result of human achievement through a steady advancement of civilization. For sure, the new world is working itself out, but in the mystery of faith, hidden from the wise of this world (1 Cor 1.19-21; 2.6-9). The kingdom, after all, is of God and not man. Nevertheless, "the messianic era initiated by the Incarnation can only be established with the collaboration of mankind. This collaboration is called synergy. We prepare for the Second Coming, the final triumph of justice and life over evil and death, by becoming united by faith to the crucified and risen Savior."[78]

Besides these shared themes, each of the three days of the Bridegroom has its own special commemoration that distinguishes it from the other two.

Great Monday

On Great Monday we commemorate Joseph the Patriarch, the beloved son of Jacob. A major figure of the Old Testament, Joseph's story is told in the final section of the Book of Genesis (chs. 37-50). Because of his exceptional qualities and remarkable life, our patristic and liturgical tradition portrays Joseph as τύπος Χριστοῦ, i.e., as a prototype, prefigurement or image of Christ. The story of Joseph illustrates the mystery of God's providence, promise and redemption. Innocent, chaste and righteous, his life bears witness to the power of God's love and promise. The lesson to be learned from Joseph's life, as it bears upon the ultimate redemption wrought by the death and resurrection of Christ, is summed up in the words he addressed to his brothers who had previously betrayed him, " 'Fear not . . . As for you, you meant evil against me; but God meant it for good, to bring about that many people should be kept alive, as they are today. So do not fear; I will provide for you and your little ones.' Thus he reassured them and comforted them" (Gen 50.19-21). The commemoration of the noble, blessed and saintly Joseph reminds us that in the great events of the Old Testament, the Church recognizes the realities of the New Testament.

Also, on Great Monday the Church commemorates the event of the cursing of the fig tree (Mt 21.18-20). In the Gospel narrative this event is said to have occured on the morrow of Jesus' triumphant entry into Jerusalem (Mt 21.18 and Mk 11.12). For this reason it found its way into the liturgy of Great Monday. The episode is also quite relevant to Great Week. Together with the event of the cleansing of the Temple this episode is another manifestation of Jesus' divine power and authority and a revelation as well of God's judgment upon the faithlessness of the Jewish religious classes. The fig tree is symbolic of Israel become barren by her failure to recognize and receive Christ and His teachings. The cursing of the fig tree is a parable in action, a symbolic gesture. Its meaning should not be lost on any one in any generation. Christ's judgment on the faithless, unbelieving, unrepentant and unloving will be certain and decisive on the Last Day. This episode makes it clear that nominal Christianity is not only inadequate, it is also despicable and unworthy of God's kingdom. Genuine Christian faith is dynamic and fruitful. It permeates one's whole being and causes a change. Living, true and unadulterated faith makes the Christian conscious of the fact that he is already a citizen of heaven. Therefore, his way of thinking, feeling, acting and being must reflect this reality. Those who belong to Christ ought to live and walk in the Spirit; and the Spirit will bear fruit in them: love, joy, peace, patience, kindness, goodness, faithfulness, gentleness, self-control (Gal 5.22-25).

Great Tuesday

On Great Tuesday the Church calls to remembrance two parables, which are related to the Second Coming. The one is the parable of the Ten Virgins (Mt 25.1-3); the other the parable of the Talents (Mt 25.14-30). These parables point to the inevitability of the Parousia and deal with such subjects as spiritual vigilance, stewardship, accountability and judgement.

From these parables we learn at least two basic things. First, Judgement Day will be like the situation in which the bridesmaids (or virgins) of the parable found themselves: some ready for it, some not ready. The time one decides for God is now and not at some undefined point in the future. If "time and tide waits for no man," certainly the Parousia is no exception. The tragedy of the closed door is that individuals close it, not God. The exclusion from the marriage feast, the kingdom is of our own making. Second, we are reminded that watchfulness and readiness do not mean a wearisome, spiritless performance of formal and empty obligations. Most certainly it does not mean inactivity and slothfulness. Watchfulness signifies inner stability, soberness, tranquility and joy. It means spiritual alertness, attentiveness and vigilance. Watchfulness is the deep personal resolve to find and do the will of God, embrace every commandment and every virtue, and guard the intellect and heart from evil thoughts and actions. Watchfulness is the intense love of God. St. Hesychios the Priest described it with these words:

> Through His incarnation God gave us the model for a holy life and recalled us from our ancient fall. In addition to many other things, He taught us, feeble as we are, that we should fight against the demons with humility, fasting, prayer and watchfulness. For when, after His baptism, he went into the desert and the devil came up to Him as though He were merely a man, He began His spiritual warfare by fasting and won the battle by this means — though, being God, and God of gods, he had no need of any such means at all.
>
> I shall now tell you in plain, straightforward language what I consider to be the types of watchfulness which gradually cleanse the

intellect from impassioned thoughts. One type of watchfulness
consists in closely scrutinizing every mental image or provoca-
tion; for only by means of a mental image can Satan fabricate
an evil thought and insinuate this into the intellect in order to
lead it astray. A second type of watchfulness consists in freeing
the heart form all thoughts, keeping it profoundly silent and still,
and in praying. A third type consists in continually and humbly
calling upon the Lord Jesus Christ for help. A fourth type is always
to have the thought of death in one's mind. These types of watchfulness, my child, act like doorkeepers and bar entry to evil
thoughts. A further type which, along with the others, is also effective is to fix one's gaze on heaven and to pay no attention
to anything material.[79]

Great Wednesday

On Great Wednesday the Church invites the faithful to focus
their attention on two figures: the sinful woman who anointed the
head of Jesus shortly before the passion (Mt 26.6-13), and Judas,
the disciple who betrayed the Lord. The former acknowledged
Jesus as Lord, while the latter severed himself from the Master.
The one was set free, while the other became a slave. The one
inherited the kingdom, while the other fell into perdition. These
two people bring before us concerns and issues related to *freedom,
sin, hell* and *repentance.* The full meaning of these things can
be understood only within the context and from the perspective
of the existential truth of our human existence.

Freedom belongs to the nature and character of a human being because he has been created in the image of God. Man and
his true life is defined by his uncreated Archtype, who, according
to the Greek Fathers, is Christ. Man's ultimate grandeur, in the
words of one theologian, "is not found in his being the highest
biological existence, a rational or political animal, but in his being a deified animal, in the fact that he constitutes a created existence which has received the command to become a god."[80] In
the final analysis, man becomes authentically free in God; in his
ability to discover, accept, pursue, enjoy and deepen the filial relationship which God confers upon him. Freedom is not something
extraneous and accidental, but intrinsic to genuine human life.

It is not a contrivance of human ingenuity and cleverness, but a divine gift. Man is free, because his being has been sealed with the image of God. He has been endowed with and possesses divine qualities. He reflects in himself God, who, someone has said, "reveals Himself as personal existence, as distinctiveness and freedom." The ultimate truth of man is found in his vocation to become a conscious personal existence; a god by grace. The elemental exercise of freedom lies in one's conscious decision and desire to fulfill his vocation to become a person or to deny it; to become a being of communion or an entity unto death; to become a saint or a devil.

Since man is able to resist God and turn away from Him, he can diminish and disfigure God's image in him to the extreme limits. He is able to misuse, abuse, distort, pervert and debase the natural powers and qualities with which he has been endowed. He is capable of sin. Sin turns him into a fraud and an impostor. It limits his life to the level of biological existence, robbing it of divine splendor and capacity. Lacking faith and moral judgement, man is capable of turning freedom into license, rebellion, intimidation and enslavement.

Sin is more than breaking rules and transgressing commandments. It is the willful rejection of a personal relationship with the living God. It is separation and alienation; a way of death, "an existence which does not come to fruition," to use the words of St. Maximos the Confessor. Sin is the denial of God and the forfeiting of heaven. It is the seduction, abduction and captivity of the soul through provocations of the devil, through pride and mindless pleasures. Sin is the light become darkness, the harbinger of hell, the eternal fire and outer darkness. "Hell," according to one theologian, "is man's free choice; it is when he imprisons himself in an agonizing lack of life, and deliberately refuses communion with the loving goodness of God, the true life."[81]

To sin is to miss the mark, to fail to realize one's vocation and destiny. Sin brings disorder and fragmentation. It diminishes life and causes the most pure and most noble parts of our nature to end up as passions, i.e., faculties and impulses that have become distorted, spoiled, violated and finally alien to the true self.

Sin is not just a disposition. It is a deliberate choice and an act. Likewise, *repentance* is not merely a change in attitude, but a choice to follow God. This choice involves a radical, existential change which is beyond our own capacity to accomplish. It is a gift bestowed by Christ, who takes us unto Himself through His Church, in order to forgive, heal and restore us to wholeness. The gift He gives us is a new and clean heart.

Having experienced this kind of reintegration, as well as the power of spiritual freedom that issues from it, we come to realize that a truly virtuous life is more than the occasional display of conventional morality. The outward impression of virtue is nothing more than conceit. True virtue is the struggle for truth and the deliberate choice of our own free will to become an imitator of Christ. Then, in the words of St. Maximos, "God who yearns for the salvation of all men and hungers after their deification, withers their self-conceit like the unfruitful fig tree. He does this so that they may prefer to be righteous in reality rather than appearance, discarding the cloak of hypocritical moral display and genuinely pursuing a virtuous life in the way that the divine Logos wishes them to. They will then live with reverence, revealing the state of their soul to God rather than displaying the external appearance of a moral life to their fellow-men."[82]

The process of healing and restoring our damaged, broken, wounded and fallen nature is on-going. God is merciful and long-suffering towards His creation. He accepts repentant sinners tenderly and rejoices in their conversion.[83] This process of conversion includes the purification and illumination of our mind and heart, so that our passions may be continually educated rather than eradicated, transfigured and not suppressed, used positively and not negatively.[84]

The act of repentance is not some kind of cheerless, morbid exercise. It is a joy-bringing event and enterprise, which frees the conscience from the burdens and anxieties of sin and makes the soul rejoice in the truth and love of God. Repentance begins with the recognition and renunciation of one's evil ways. From this interior sorrow it proceeds to the verbal acknowledgement of the concrete sins before God and the witness of the Church.[85] By "becoming conscious both of his own sinfulness and of the forgiveness extended to him by God," the repentant sinner turns freely towards God in an attitude of love and trust. Then he focuses his truest and deepest self, his heart, continually on Christ, in order to become like Him. Experiencing the embracing love of God as freedom and transfiguration (2 Cor 3.17-18), he authenticates his own personal existence and shows heartfelt concern, compassion and love for others.

I have transgressed more than the harlot, O loving Lord, yet never have I offered You my flowing tears. But in silence I fall down before You and with love I kiss Your most pure feet, beseeching You as Master to grant me remission of sins; and I cry to You, O Savior: Deliver me from the filth of my works.

While the sinful woman brought oil of myrrh, the disciple came to an agreement with the transgressors. She rejoiced to pour out what was very precious, he made haste to sell the One who is above all price. She acknowledged Christ as Lord, he severed himself from the Master. She was set free, but Judas became the slave of the enemy. Grievous was his lack of love. Great was her repentance. Grant such repentance also unto me, O Savior who has suffered for our sake, and save us.

(Orthros of Great Wednesday)

GENERAL OBSERVATIONS

Vestments — The tone of Great Week is particularly solemn, somber and mournful. This mood is reflected in the way the Church is lit, as well as in the vestments worn by the clergy and the cover that adorns the holy Table. The Church is lit dimly. At the solemn processions the congregation usually holds candles. According to ancient practice and custom the clergy wear black vestments and the holy Table is covered with a black cloth. However, in many places today the color black has been replaced by deep purple. *The Icon* displayed for veneration during the first three days is the icon of the Νυμφίος — Bridegroom.[86]

The Apolysis for each divine service is the same for all of the three days. It has a special prologue, which reads as follows: "'Ερχόμενος ὁ Κύριος ἐπὶ τὸ ἑκούσιον Πάθος διὰ τὴν ἡμῶν σωτηρίαν, Χριστὸς

ὁ ἀληθινὸς Θεὸς ἡμῶν . . . — May the Lord who comes to His voluntary passion for our salvation, Christ our true God . . .''

The Katzion — In the beginning of the Orthros service[87] at the
appointed time the priest uses the hand censer known as the
Katzion[88] to cense the Church. The regular censer is used at all
other times.

The Service — Each day of Great Week includes all of the services of the daily cycle of worship. The order and material for
these services is found in the Triodion, and the Patriarchal Text.
It is found as well in the Lenten Triodion. In current parish usage,
however, the daily services are usually limited to the Vespers with
the Pre-Sanctified Liturgy and the Orthros. The basic structure
of these services is patterned after the order of the Lenten weekday services. Except for the obvious variations in the troparia
(hymns) and Scripture lessons, the order of the divine services is
the same for all of the three days. The Orthros of these days is
usually referred to as the Service of the Bridegroom — 'Ακολουθία
τοῦ Νυμφίου.

The Pre-Sanctified Divine Liturgy

This Liturgy is celebrated on the first three days of Great Week.
In some parishes, however, the Liturgy is celebrated only on Great
Wednesday for practical reasons.

The Liturgy of the Pre-Sanctified Gifts has a distinct character
and order.[89] It is comprised of three major parts or components:
a) the service of Great Vespers peculiar to this Liturgy; b) the
solemn transfer of the Pre-Sanctified Gifts to the holy Table; and
c) the preparation for and the distribution of holy Communion.
The Liturgy does not contain the Anaphora,[90] the Gifts of the
bread and wine having been consecrated at the Divine Liturgy
on the previous Sunday or Saturday.

The Liturgy of the Pre-Sanctified developed over a long period
of time. Though its history and structure is complex, its origins
can be traced to two customs of the early Church. The first is
related to the practice of self-communion, i.e., the private communion at home of the consecrated holy Bread, received previously
at the Sunday Liturgy.[91] The second is related to the rules

regulating the practice of fasting.

It was customary in the early Church for many Christians, clerics, laity and ascetics alike, to receive holy Communion daily in their homes. The consecrated Gifts were distributed for this purpose at the Sunday Eucharist to those who desired them. Though this practice was discontinued, it provided the impetus for the creation of a new form of Communion, i.e., the distribution and Communion of the reserved sacrament in the context of a communal worship service.

With regard to the rules and customs pertaining to fasting, two practices are of special significance in the development of the Liturgy of the Pre-Sanctified. In the early Church Wednesdays and Fridays were observed with a total fast, which meant complete abstinence from food and drink until the late afternoon. The practice was especially true for Great Lent.[92] The total fast signified both the spiritual concentration and expectation of an approaching joy as well as the last and ultimate preparation for a decisive spiritual event and feast.[93] For this reason a total fast was observed also in preparation for holy Communion.[94]

The second practice is related to the celebration of the Eucharist. From early times it was considered inappropriate to celebrate the Eucharist on fast days.[95] The reason for this is based on the understanding of the Eucharist as the feast of the Church. In as much as the celebration of the Eucharist constitutes a feast, it is incompatible with fasting.[96] While fasting signifies the way toward the fullness, the Eucharist is the manifestation of that fullness.

The combination of these factors resulted in the development of the Liturgy of the Pre-Sanctified, which can be defined succinctly as: the distribution and communion of the reserved sacrament at the end of a fast day in the context of a communal worship service, consisting mainly of Vespers and elements of the Divine Liturgy.

The Liturgy of the Pre-Sanctified Gifts enjoyed wider and more frequent use in earlier times. Besides the Great Lent and the first three days of Great Week, it was celebrated also on Wednesdays and Fridays throughout the year, on Great Friday and on the Feast of the Exaltation of the Cross.[97]

The Liturgy of the Pre-Sanctified Gifts, in addition to manifesting vividly the spirit of joyous-sorrow (χαρμολύπη) which characterizes the Lenten Season and Great Week, serves to highlight an important aspect of our eucharistic theology. The eucharistic elements of the bread and wine once consecrated continue to be the life giving Body and Blood of Christ, given to the faithful as communion for the forgiveness of sins and life eternal.[98]

The Mystery of Holy Unction (Εὐχέλαιον)

The Mystery of Holy Unction[99] is established upon the words and actions of our Lord Jesus Christ. It embodies, extends and continues His healing ministry. It is the sign of His transforming presence in a bruised and hurting world, and the emblem of His promise to deliver us from sin and corruption. It is the manifestation of the kingdom and the sign of what God has in store for the world when it reaches its state of ultimate completion.

Sickness and death are inescapable indignities resulting from the Fall. These indignities are not forms of divine retribution, but the result of the world's deep alienation from God. He allows death to terminate graceless life, not as punishment, but so that it may be restored to its fullness in the resurrection.

Christ took our infirmities and bore our diseases (Mt 8.17). He overcame the world and has given humanity access to imperishable life. The sacrament of Holy Unction places the sick person into this eschatological reality, where suffering, corruption and death are overcome.

Holy Unction is a sacrament of faith (Jas 5.14-15). It is meant for any sick person and is always celebrated in the hope that it will bring healing. While this certainly is the desired effect, it is not the indispensable condition of the sacrament. The essential purpose of the sacrament is to allow the person to share in the victory of Christ and to raise him into the realm of God's Kingdom. It communicates spiritual power so that the trials of sickness may be borne with courage, hope and fortitude. The sacrament is not a substitute for medical treatment. In time of illness, we are guided by the words of Scripture: "When you are sick do not be negligent but pray to the Lord and He will heal you . . . And give the physician his place, for the Lord created him" (Sirach 38.9-10).

The Sacrament may be celebrated at any time for the sick. It is celebrated with special solemnity on Great Wednesday for the entire community for the healing of the spiritual and bodily infirmities of the faithful. Through the prayer of its priest, the congregation asks God for forgiveness, help and deliverance from the cycle of sin and suffering.[100] The borders between the sickness of the body and the sickness of the soul are not always strictly defined. Because we cannot draw a sharp distinction between bodily and spiritual illness, the Church confers Holy Unction upon all the faithful whether they are physically ill or not.

The solemn celebration of Holy Unction on Great Wednesday serves to remind the faithful of Christ's power to forgive and liberate the conscience from the blight of personal and collective sin. Thus, it helps emphasize the glorious expectation of Pascha: the resurrection, redemption and sanctification of all life. In addition, it helps the faithful to realize how fragile human life really is and how dependent we are on God, if life is to have any true meaning and purpose. The sacrament also helps us to know that the integration of the human personality and the restoration of interior justice and holiness are basic presuppositions for healing. The corporate celebration should remind us also that caring for the sick and the afflicted, and comforting them in their distress and plight is both a personal as well as a communal responsibility. Finally, the sacrament helps us to recall that the defeat of suffering, sickness and death — the indignities of the ancestral sin — can be understood only in the light of Christ's own death and resurrection.

It is not altogether clear how and when the Sacrament of Holy Unction came to be celebrated on Great Wednesday. it may be related to the fact that in Christian antiquity penitents were received and reconciled during the course of Great Week. The sacrament of Holy Unction may have been part of the reception process for lapsed Christians, who were reconciled to the Church through the sacrament of Penance.

It has become the practice among the Greek Orthodox in the United States to conduct the sacrament on Great Wednesday evening in the place of the usual service of the Triodion. Pastoral considerations have dictated this custom.[101]

The service of Holy Unction is found in the Euchologion. It is contained also in the Holy Week Book edited by Fr. George Papadeas. In its basic structure the service contains the following parts: a modified Orthros; a prayer for the consecration of the oil; a set of seven Scripture lessons, each with an Epistle and Gospel pericope and a priestly prayer; and finally, an additional prayer for the anointing of the person(s) for whom the sacrament is celebrated.[102]

RUBRICS

The rubrics contained in this section are for the service of the Orthros. As it was noted above, the rubrics for the Liturgy of the Pre-Sanctified are contained elsewhere. For the service of the Hours the reader may refer to the Triodion or the Patriarchal Text. The order of these latter services is straightforward.

Except for the variations in the hymns and the Scripture Lessons, the order of the Orthros is the same for all of the three first days of Great Week. For this reason it is sufficient to mention only the rubrics of the Orthros of the first day, Great Monday.

With the Orthros of Great Monday we begin the reversed position of the order of the services. Thus, the Orthros of Great Monday is celebrated in the evening of Palm Sunday.

The Orthros of Great Monday
  Opening Doxology and Imperial Office.[103]
  The Priest — stands, as usual, before the Holy Table and says: "Εὐλογητὸς ὁ Θεὸς ἡμῶν . . . — Blessed is our God . . .''; "Δόξα σοι ὁ Θεός . . . — Glory to You, o God . . .''; and the "Βασιλεῦ οὐράνιε — Heavenly King.''[104]
  People — recite the Trisagion prayers.
  Chanter — intones the Royal Psalms (19, 20). At this time the priest censes the entire Church with the katzion.[105] Before commencing the censing the priest wears the phelonion.

People — repeat the Trisagion at the end of the psalms and then recite the Royal troparia.

Priest — intones the abbreviated fervent litany.

Enarxis.

Reader — says, "In the Name of the Lord, Father bless."

Priest — says, "Δόξα τῇ ἁγίᾳ . . . — Glory to the . . ." (and proceeds to read the prescribed prayers in a low voice before the Holy Table).

Reader — recites the Hexapsalmos (Six-Psalms).[106]

Priest — intones the Great Synapte.

People — sing the Alleluia with the four verses (Is 26.9,10,11,15), and the troparion "'Ιδοὺ ὁ Νυμφίος — Behold the Bridegroom" (thrice).

Procession — As the troparion is being sung, the priest carries the icon of the Νυμφίος — Bridegroom in procession in the usual manner.[107] This procession is conducted only once, at the Orthros of Great Monday. The icon remains in the usual place for the first three days of the week.

The Kathismata

When the hymn "Behold the Bridegroom" has been sung three times, the Priest intones the Small Litany. The people respond in the usual manner.

The reading of a section or Kathisma of the Psalter follows.[108] However, for reasons of brevity it had long become the practice to suppress the recitation of the Psalter in parish usuage. A set of hymns follows the recitation of each Kathisma. These hymns are called καθίσματα τροπάρια — sessional hymns. The sessional hymns have remained in use and are sung in their usual place. Thus, after the Priest has intoned the Small Litany the chanters and people sing the sessional hymns.

The Gospel

Following the kathismata or sessional hymns the Priest reads the prescribed pericope of the Gospel.[109] The Lesson is preceded by the usual liturgical formula. The Gospel is read from the Holy Gate.[110]

Psalm 50

When the reading of the Gospel has been completed the Reader recites Psalm 50 (51).

The Canon

After this, the chanters and the people sing the appointed Odes of the Canon. The Reader recites the Kontakion and Oikos of the Triodion, as well as the Synaxarion of the Menaion and the Triodion. The Priest intones the Small Litany at the prescribed interval.

When the Katavasia of the Eighth Ode has been chanted, the Priest says, "Τὴν Θεοτόκον — Let us magnify" and censes the sanctuary and the people in the usual manner.

The chanters and people sing the hymns of the Ninth Ode.

The Priest intones the Small Litany at the conclusion of the Ninth Ode.

The Exaposteilarion and Ainoi

Then the chanters and people sing the Exaposteilarion "Τὸν νυμφῶνα σου βλέπω — I see Thy bridle-chamber" three times.[111]

This is followed by the singing of the Psalms of Praise (148, 149, 150) together with the designated hymns, concluding with the Doxastikon.[112]

The Doxology

The reader and the people recite the so-called Small Doxology.[113]

The Petitions

At the conclusion of the Doxology the Priest intones the petitions. He gives the Peace and reads the Prayer of Inclination.

The Aposticha Hymns

The chanters and the people sing the appointed Aposticha.

The Apolysis[114]

The Priest recites the "'Αγαθὸν τὸ ἐξομολογεῖσθαι τῷ Κυρίῳ . . . — It is a good thing to give thanks . . ."

The people recite the trisagion prayers; Lord, have mercy (12); and say "Father bless."

The Priest says the following:

1)'Ο "Ων Εὐλογητός . . . — Blessed is He Who Is . . ."

2)'Επουράνιε Βασιλεῦ . . . — Heavenly King . . ."

3)The prayer of St. Ephraim accompanied by the usual deep prostrations.

4)The Apolysis: "'Ερχόμενος ὁ Κύριος . . ."

Chapter Three

Great Thursday

COMMENTS ON THE MAIN THEMES

On Great Thursday the focus of the Church turns to the events that occurred in the Upper Room and at the Garden of Gethsemane.

In the Upper Room, while at meal, Jesus established and instituted the mystery or sacrament of the holy Eucharist and washed the feet of His disciples as well.

The Garden of Gethsemane calls our attention to Jesus' redemptive obedience and sublime prayer (Mt 26.36-46). It also brings us before the cowardly, treacherous act of Judas, who betrayed Christ with a kiss, the sign of love and friendship.

The Eucharist[115]

At the Mystical Supper in the Upper Room Jesus gave a radically new meaning to the food and drink of the sacred meal. He identified Himself with the bread and wine: "Take, eat; this is my Body. . . Drink of it all of you; for this is my Blood of the New Covenant" (Mt 26.26-28).

We have learned to equate food with life because it sustains our earthly existence. In the Eucharist the distinctively unique human food — bread and wine — becomes our gift of life. Consecrated and sanctified, the bread and wine become the Body and Blood of Christ. This change is not physical but mystical and sacramental. While the qualities of the bread and wine remain, we partake of the true Body and Blood of Christ. In the eucharistic meal God enters into such a communion of life that He feeds humanity with His own being, while still remaining distinct. In the words of St. Maximos the Confessor, Christ, "transmits to us divine life, making Himself eatable." The Author of life shatters the limitations of our createdness. Christ acts so that "we might become sharers of divine nature" (2 Pet 1.4).

The Eucharist is at the center of the Church's life. It is her

51

most profound prayer and principal activity. It is at one and the
same time both the source and the summit of her life. In the
Eucharist the Church manifests her true nature and is continuously
changed from a human community into the Body of Christ, the
Temple of the Holy Spirit, and the People of God.

The Eucharist is the pre-eminent sacrament. It completes all
the others and recapitulates the entire economy of salvation. Our
new life in Christ is constantly renewed and increased by the
Eucharist. The Eucharist imparts life and the life it gives is the
life of God.[116]

Through baptism and chrismation we have entered into a new
mode of existence. It is an existence of constant becoming. The
Scriptures describe this as new birth, the death of the old man,
the putting off of the old nature and the putting on of the
new.[117] This newness, this radical change in the mode of existence, is not accomplished by human effort. It is a gift from God.
Rooted in the age to come, this new existence is maintained and
nourished by the Eucharist. At every Divine Liturgy we hear the
good news of Christ and enter into the process of conversion. We
are given the possibility to acquire for ourselves the eucharistic
manner of existence. Little by little we become ourselves communion and love. At the Divine Liturgy the tragic elements of our
fallen existence — pride, individualism, blasphemy, vanity,
hypocricy, envy, anger, division, fear, despair, pain, deceit, un-
truth, malice, greed, vice, gluttony, passions, corruption, death —
are being continuously defeated, in order to make us capable to
be love, freedom and life.[118]

The Eucharist is offered to the Church as a whole not as a
reward, but as a remedy for sin, a provision for life, the communion of the Holy Spirit, and an opening to others. Every baptized
and chrismated Orthodox Christian should be a regular and frequent recipient of the divine Mysteries. Care, however, must be
taken that Holy Communion is approached with spiritual discernment and adequate preparation. A total fast, as described above,
precedes our reception of Holy Communion. The observance of
God's commandments constitutes the essential preparation and
proper disposition for participation in the sacrament.[119]

In the Eucharist the Church remembers and enacts sacramentally the redemtive event of the Cross and participates in its saving grace. This does not suggest that the Eucharist attempts to reclaim a past event. The Eucharist does not repeat what cannot be repeated. Christ is not slain anew and repeatedly. Rather the eucharistic food is changed concretely and really into the Body and Blood of the Lamb of God, "Who gave Himself up for the life of the world."[120] Christ, the Theanthropos, continually offers Himself to the faithful through the consecrated Gifts, i.e., His very own risen and deified Body, which for our sake died once and now lives (Heb 10.2; Rev 1.18). Hence, the faithful come to Church week by week not only to worship God and to hear His word. They come, first of all, to experience over and over the mystery of salvation and to be united intimately to the Passion and Resurrection of the Lord Jesus Christ.

By the power of His sacrifice Christ draws us into His own sacrificial action. The Church also offers sacrifice. However, the sacrifice offered by the Church and her members can only be an offering given in return to God on account of the riches of His goodness, mercy and love. This sacrifice is first of all, a sacrifice of praise and thanksgiving. It also has other forms, including commitment to the Gospel, loyalty to the true faith, constant prayer, fasting, struggles against the passions, and works of charity. At its deepest level, however, this offering in return (ἀντιπροσφορά) is an act of kenosis (Lk 9.23-25). It is constituted by our willingness to lose our life in order to gain it (Mt 16.28).

In the Eucharist we receive and partake of the resurrected Christ. We share in His sacrificed, risen and deified Body, "for the forgiveness of sins and life eternal" (Divine Liturgy). In the Eucharist Christ pours into us — as a permanent and constant gift — the Holy Spirit, "Who bears witness with our spirit that we are children of God — and if children — then heirs with Christ (Rom 8.16-17).

The central fruit of the Eucharist is the communion of the Holy Spirit. The Holy Spirit is the Giver of Life, who prepares us for the resurrection and makes us advance toward it (Rom 8.2, 9-8). The other fruits of the Eucharist are related to this central gift.

Vigilance of soul, forgiveness of sins, a clear conscience are both
a preparation for as well as the result of our communion with the
Holy Spirit. Sonship, fellowhip with the saints, the manifestation
of love in the unity of faith, and the inheritance of the heavenly
kingdom are obtained by the communion of the Holy Spirit.

St. Gregory Palamas, in an insightful passage, helps us to
understand the profound power and wonder of the Eucharist:

> Christ has become our brother by sharing our flesh and blood
> and so becoming assimilated to us . . . He has joined and bound
> us to Himself, as a husband his wife, by becoming one single flesh
> with us through the communion of His blood; He has also become
> our Father by divine baptism which renders us like unto Him,
> and He nourishes us at His own breast as a tender mother
> nourishes her babies . . . Come, He says, eat my Body, drink my
> Blood . . . so that you be not only made after God's image, but
> become gods and kings, eternal and heavenly, clothing yourselves
> with me, King and God.[121]

The Washing of the Feet

The events initiated by Jesus at the Mystical Supper were profoundly significant. By teaching and giving the disciples His final
instructions and praying for them as well, He revealed again His
divine Sonship and authority. By establishing the Eucharist, He
enshrines to perfection God's most intimate purposes for our salvation, offering Himself as Communion and life. By washing the feet
of His disciples, he summarized the meaning of His ministry,
manifested His perfect love and revealed His profound humility.

The act of the washing of the feet (Jn. 13:2-17) is closely related
to the sacrifice of the Cross. Both reveal aspects of Christ's kenosis.
While the cross constitues the ultimate manifestation of Christ's
perfect obedience to His Father (Phil 2.5-8), the washing of the
feet signifies His intense love and the giving of Himself to each
person according to that person's ability to receive Him (Jn 13.6-9).

In a meditation on liturgical and priestly service, Father Lev
Gillet — who wrote under the pseudonym A Monk of the Eastern
Church — made the following observations on the significance of
Jesus' act. Though his words are addressed to priests, they are

appropriate for and applicable to every Christian as well.

The washing of feet does not merely signify a necessary purification — take away the dust accumulated along the roadway, take
away the errors due to human weakness. More than that, this act
is a mystery of humility and love. Jesus wanted to be designated
by the prophet Isaiah as the "Suffering Servant." In the Gospels
He describes Himself as "Him who serves." He insisted on the
fact that, in the Kingdom of God, the greatest should be the least.
And now, before entering into His Passion, he says to His disciples:
"If I, your Lord and Teacher, have washed your feet, you also
ought to wash one another's feet. For I have given you an example, that you also should do as I have done to you" (Jn 13.14-15).

The priest of Jesus cannot fruitfully accomplish this double priestly
act — share the bread of the Word and break the bread of the
Lord's Supper — unless, first of all, like His master, he kneels
before others in an attitude of humility and service, and washes
their feet. Without this precondition, his ministry will bear no
fruit. How, then, in the priest's daily life, can this attitude of
humility and service be realized?

Every pastoral act performed by the priest and every human relationship established by him should be marked by this double attitude of humility and service . . . Above all other, the priest should
devote himself to those who suffer . . . For the task of the priest
is to direct towards the Savior every form of physical or
psychological suffering, as well as every need for salvation. The
priest will be especially devoted to the dying, the sick, those in
prison, the persecuted, the poor, and the afflicted. He will give
alms in the form of his money and his consolation. If he has no
money, he will recall the words St. Peter spoke to the paralytic,
and say: "I have neither silver nor gold, but I give you what I
have . . ." (Acts 3.6). What I have — that is, my affection and
my prayer . . . In each new situation the priest is called upon
to make a wholly new effort of understanding and love . . . The
priest has done nothing until he himself has "shared" the burden
borne by the other person, until he himself has tried to bear that
same burden (in a way that differs in each case and should be
guided by discernment and grace), until he himself has truly
entered into the suffering of his brother, and until his compas-

sion actually costs him something and directs him towards a specific sacrifice.[122]

Prayer

The Synoptic Gospels have preserved for us another significant episode in the series of events leading to the Passion, namely, the agony and prayer of Jesus in the Garden of Gethsemane (Mt 26.36-46; Mk. 14.32-42; Lk. 22.39-46).

Although Jesus was Son of God, He was destined as man to accept fully the human condition, to experience suffering and to learn obedience. Divesting Himself of divine prerogatives, the Son of God assumed the role of a servant. He lived a truly human existence. Though He was Himself sinless, He allied Himself with the whole human race, identified with the human predicament, and experienced the same tests (Phil 2.6-11; Heb 2.9-18).

The moving events in the Garden of Gethsemane dramatically and poignantly disclosed the human nature of Christ. The sacrifice He was to endure for the salvation of the world was imminent. Death, with all its brutal force and fury, stared directly at Him. Its terrible burden and fear — the calamitous results of the ancestral sin — caused Him intense sorrow and pain (Heb 5.7). Instinctively, as man He sought to escape it. He found Himself in a moment of decision. In His agony He prayed to His Father, "Abba, Father, all things are possible to thee; remove this cup from me; yet not what I will, but what thou wilt" (Mk 14.36).

His prayer revealed the depths of His agony and sorrow. It revealed as well His "incomparable spiritual strength (and) immovable desire and decision . . . to bring about the will of the Father."[123]

Jesus offered His unconditional love and trust to the Father. He reached the extreme limits of self denial — "not what I will" — in order to accomplish His Father's will. His acceptance of death was not some kind of stoic passivity and resignation but an act of absolute love and obedience. In that moment of decision, when He declared His acceptance of death to be in agreement with the Father's will, he broke the power of the fear of death with all its attending uncertainties, anxieties and limitations. He learned obedience and fulfilled the divine plan (Heb 5.8-9).

In the course of His agony, Jesus exhorted His disciples to watch and pray that they may not enter into temptation (Mt 26.41). This same admonition is applicable to every Christian in every generation.

Prayer connects us with Jesus, who, through His obedience became the unique and perfect worshipper of God. He becomes both the model as well as the subject of our prayer. Thus, with Christ always on our mind and in our heart we can neither be tempted nor can we perish, to paraphrase an ancient Christian text.[124]

Prayer is the power that fuels the spiritual life. As breathing, eating, drinking, and thinking are essential to human existence, prayer is a fundamental element and acitivity of the Christian life. Authentic Orthodox spirituality is constituted by a vibrant prayer life rooted in the life of the Church, her faith and her sacraments; and related, as well, to the practice of fasting, which is seen primarily as obedience to and love for God, the transformation of the passions, and acts of charity.

Prayer is the most sublime experience of the human soul. Without it the soul is left cold and spiritless. It cannot enter into a sustained personal relationship with God.

Prayer is an act of faith. It brings us to the threshold of another world. Through it we reach and cross the ultimate frontier. We touch another world, which we come to experience as extraordinary peace, beauty, goodness, joy and trust. Prayer opens our life to a new reality which transcends us. We encounter the living God and converse with Him. The Holy One, who alone has existence, embraces us with His tender mercy, compassion and love. Divine light penetrates the depths of our soul to reveal our sins, purge our iniquities, heal our brokenness, illumine our intellect, strengthen our will, and gladden our heart.

The Betrayal

As we noted above, Judas betrayed Christ with a kiss, the sign of friendship and love. The betrayal and crucifixion of Christ carried the ancestral sin to its exteme limits. In these two acts the rebellion against God reached its maximum capacity. The seduction of man in paradise culminated in the death of God in the flesh. To be victorious evil must quench the light and discredit the good. In the end, however, it shows itself to be a lie, an absurdity and sheer madness. The death and resurrection of Christ rendered evil powerless.

On Great Thursday light and darkness, joy and sorrow are so stangely mixed. At the Upper Room and in Gethsemane the light of the kingdom and the darkness of hell come through simultaneously. The way of life and the way of death converge. We meet them both in our journey through life.

Everyone born into this life is involved inevitably in the spiritual warfare, contending not against flesh and blood, "but against the principalities, against the powers, against the world rulers of this present darkness, against the spiritual hosts of wickedness" (Eph 6.12).

Sadly, there are those who continue in willful disobedience, who not only reject God but also wage war upon Him. There are others who evade Him. And still others, who have been baptized, but for one reason or another are negligent or lukewarm in their relationship with Christ and His Church.

In the midst of the snares and temptations that abound in the world around and in us we must be eager to live in communion with everything that is good, noble, natural, and sinless, forming ourselves by God's grace in the likeness of Christ.

GENERAL OBSERVATIONS

Holy Chrism

In Christian antiquity it was customary to baptize the catechumens on the feast of Pascha. The oils of Chrism, used for the anointing of the neophytes or newly-baptized persons, were consecrated in advance, on Great Thursday. This practice continued through the late middle ages. The service of consecration was conducted annually. In time, however, it began to be celebrated occasionally, as the need to replace the Chrism arose.

When it is performed, the long and elaborate service takes place at the conclusion of the Divine Liturgy on Great Thursday.

By ancient practice and custom the right to consecrate the Chrism belongs only to the bishop, although presbyters usually administer it in current usage. Each autocephalous church has the right to prepare and consecrate holy Chrism. The Patriarchate of Constantinople, as the first see of Orthodoxy, consecrates and distributes holy Chrism to other churches.

Holy Chrism is also called holy Myron. It is a mixture of olive oil, balsam, wine and some forty aromatic substances symbolizing the fulness of sacramental grace, the sweetness of the Christian life, and the manifold and diverse gifts of the Holy Spirit.

Chrismation as the second sacrament of the Church, is related intimately to baptism both theologically and liturgically. While baptism make us sharers in Christ's death and incorporates us into His new risen existence, Chrismation makes us partakers of the Holy Spirit. Chrismation takes us beyond the restoration of our fallen nature by introducing in us the charismatic life. The Holy Spirit comes to dwell in us; embrace our life with power and love; infuse in us the gift of action; render us strong combatants in the spiritual warfare; and purify our hearts, transforming us continuously into a temple of the living God.

The Reserved Sacrament

By custom we consecrate two Lambs[125] at the Divine Liturgy on Great Thursday. The second Lamb is used as the Reserved Sacrament. The Reserved Sacrament is used especially to give communion to the sick.

The priest prepares the consecrated Lamb, which is to be reserved, in exactly the same way the Lamb is prepared and reserved for the Liturgy of the Pre-Sanctified Gifts. Special care must be taken to dry the Lamb thoroughly. To accomplish this, the Lamb is separated into several pieces. Some priests choose to heat the particles by placing them over fire (heat) in an appropriate vessel.

While there is no special service for the preparation of the Pre-Sanctified Reserved Sacrament, we have learned by tradition to do the following: At an appropriate, quiet time within the first or second day, when the Lamb has dried thoroughly, the priest approaches the holy Table and unfolds the antimension. Vested with rason and epitrachelion, he reverences in the usual manner and censes the Gifts. He places the discos or any other container that holds the Lamb, upon the antimension. Then with the lance (λόγχη) or some other appropriate instrument, he begins to break the Lamb into small particles (μερίδες), known also in the liturgical language as μαργαρίται (pearls). These are then placed in the Artophorion in an appropriate container. It is understood, that the priest performs this service with a prayerful disposition.

The Reserved Sacrament from the previous year, is consumed by the priest after the Liturgy on either Great Thursday or Great Saturday in the usual manner.

In the event the Reserved Sacrament has been exhausted; or for any reason altered, lost or destroyed; or does not exist, as in the case of the founding of a new church, the priest may consecrate a second Lamb at any Divine Liturgy, and prepare it in the manner described above, and place it in the Artophorion.

The Service of the Nipter (Washing of the Feet)
It appears that the Church had a ceremony of the Washing of the Feet annually on Great Thursday in imitation of the event at the Last Supper. For the most part, it was limited to Cathedral Churches and certain monasteries. In time, the service fell into disuse except in certain areas. It is now being recovered by many dioceses throughout the Orthodox world. The service is elaborate, dramatic and moving. It is conducted with special solemnity at the Patriarchate of Jerusalem and at the Monastery of St. John the Theologian on the island of Patmos. The service is contained in a separate liturgical book.

* * *

Vestments — Because we commemorate the establishment of the Eucharist, the usual mourning colors are not used at the Divine Liturgy on Great Thursday. The priest wears crimson or white-purple vestments. The holy Table also is covered with a similar cloth.
The Icon — On Great Thursday morning and afternoon, we display the icon of the Mystical Supper.

Fasting — Because we commemorate the establishment of the Mystery of the Eucharist, wine and oil are served at the meal of the day.

Paschal Eggs — By custom, the paschal eggs are boiled in red dye on this day. By custom too, the paschal eggs are distributed to the faithful after the Liturgy at Pascha and are served at the paschal meal(s). Of course it should be noted that this subject is a matter of custom and not a liturgical rule.

The Orthros — of Great Thursday is usually chanted the previous evening by anticipation. Sometimes it is said on the morning of the same day. However, in this country the tendency has been to ommit it. For the most part it has fallen into disuse. In its place parish clergy celebrate the service of Holy Unction.[126]

The Divine Liturgy — of Great Thursday was originally celebrated with great solemnity in the evening, in imitation of the Last Supper. In Constantinople it was preceded by the Service of the Nipter (Νιπτήρ) or Foot-washing Ceremony which was conducted by the Patriarch himself.[127]

Gradually, the Divine Liturgy was moved first to the late afternoon and later to the morning hours of the day. The Liturgy, however, has retained its original vesperal character. It is comprised of two main parts: (a) the service of the Great Vespers, including the Entrance and three Old Testament Readings, and (b) the Divine Liturgy of St. Basil, beginning with the Prayer of the Trisagion.

Great Thursday Evening — Following closely the New Testament events the solemnities of Great Thursday proper ended with the celebration of the vesperal Divine Liturgy. But as we have noted above the evening Divine Liturgies were transposed gradually to the morning hours of the day. In modern liturgical practice the Orthros of Great Friday is now celebrated on Great Thursday evening.

RUBRICS

The Order of the Vesperal Divine Liturgy
The Proskomide — The priest prepares for the Divine Liturgy in

the usual manner. At the Proskomide he will extract a second Lamb
exactly as is done for a Pre-Sanctified Liturgy.

The Vesper Service
The priest, fully vested, comes before the Holy Table in the usual
manner. He raises the Gospel and intones the enarxis, "Εὐλογημένη
ἡ Βασιλεία . . . — Blessed is the Kingdom . . ."
The Reader says "Come, let us worship. . ." and reads Psalm 103.
The Priest intones the Great Synapte.
The Choirs sing the Psalms of Vespers together with the appointed
troparia of the Triodion.
The Priest censes as usual.
The Entrance — When the choirs sing the Doxastikon hymn, the
priest reads the prayer of the Entrance of the Vespers. The Entrance
is made with the Gospel (According to an ancient custom he may
also hold the censer.). He blesses the Entrance. At the conclusion
of the hymn, he raises the Gospel and says "Σοφία. 'Ορθοί." The
Evening Song of Thanksgiving, "Φῶς ἱλαρόν — O Joyous Light,"
is sung. The priest enters the sanctuary.
The Priest says: "'Εσπέρας" at the conclusion of the hymn.
The Reader chants the Prokeimena and according to custom intones the three appointed lections of the Old Testament.

The Divine Liturgy
The Priest says "Τοῦ Κυρίου δεηθῶμεν — Let us pray to the Lord"
at the conclusion of the Old Testament readings. The Prayer of the
Trisagion follows.
The Choir sings the Trisagion hymn ("Ἅγιος ὁ Θεός — Holy God").
The Reader recites the Apostolos in the prescribed manner.
The Priest reads the Gospel.[128]
       The remainder of the Divine Liturgy of St. Basil follows. It is
celebrated in the prescribed manner. However, in the place of the
usual Cherubikon we sing the ancient troparion "Τοῦ δείπνου σου
τοῦ μυστικοῦ — At Your Mystical Supper . . ."[129] Also, this same
hymn is chanted as the Communion hymn and in the place
of "Εἴδομεν τὸ φῶς — We have seen the true light." The Apolysis
of the Divine Liturgy has a distinct festal prologue, "Ὁ δι'
ὑπερβάλλουσαν ἀγαθότητα — . . . of His exceeding goodness."

Chapter Four

Great Friday

COMMENTS ON THE MAIN THEMES

On Great Friday the Church remembers the ineffable mystery of Christ's death. Death — tormenting, indiscriminate, universal — casts its cruel shadow over all creation. It is the silent companion of life. It is present in everything, ready to stifle and impose limits upon all things. The fear of death causes anguish and despair. It shackles us to the appearances of life and makes rebellion and sin erupt in us (Heb 2.14-15).

The Scriptures assure us that "God did not make death, and He does not delight in the death of the living, for He created all things that they might exist . . . But through the devil's envy death entered the world" (Wisdom 1.13-14; 2.24). The same divinely inspired author also writes, "God created man for incorruption and made him in the image of His own eternity . . . But ungodly men by their words and deeds summoned death" (Wisdom 2.23; 1.16).

Death is an abomination, the final indignity, the ultimate enemy. It is not of God but of men. Death is the natural fruit of the old Adam who alienated himself from the source of life and made death a universal destiny, whose very fear perpetuates the agony of sin. "It was through one man that sin entered the world and through sin death, and thus death pervaded the whole human race" (Rom 5.12).

The day of Christ's death is the day of sin. The sin which polluted God's creation from the breaking dawn of time reached its frightful climax on the hill of Golgotha. There sin and evil, destruction and death came into their own. Ungodly men had Him nailed to the cross, in order to destroy Him. However, His death condemned irrevocably the fallen world by revealing its true and abnormal nature.

In Christ, who is the New Adam, there is no sin. And, therefore, there is no death. He accepted death because He assumed the whole tragedy of our life. He chose to pour His life into death, in order to destroy it; and in order to break the hold of evil. His death is the final and ultimate revelation of His perfect obedience and love. He suffered for us the excruciating pain of absolute solitude and alienation — "My God, my God, why hast Thou forsaken Me!" (Mk 15.34). Then, He accepted the ultimate horror of death with the agonizing cry, "It is finished" (Jn 19.30). His cry was at one and the same time an indication that He was in control of His death and that His work of redemtion was accomplished, finished, fulfilled. How strange! While our death is radical unfulfillment, His is total fulfillment.

Jesus did not come to meet death with an array of philosophical theories, empty prouncements or vague hopes. He met death in person, face to face. He broke the iron grip of this ancient enemy by the awesome business of dying and living again. He chased away its oppressive darkness and cruel shadows by penetrating the bottomless abysses of hell. He cracked the fortress of death and led its captives to the limitless expanses of true life.

Millenia ago Job, a just and noble man who suffered untold misery, asked this question: "If a man dies, shall he live again?" (Job 14.14). Ages passed before this fundamental question received an authentic answer. Many offered theories, but no one spoke with authority. The answer came from the One who stood by the still bodies of two young people — Jairus' daughter and the widow's only son — and raised them from the dead (Lk 8.41 and 7.11). The anwser came from the One who approached the tomb of His friend Lazaros who had been dead for four days and called him from death to life (Jn 11). The answer came from Jesus, who was Himself on route to His own ugly death on the Cross and who rose on the third day.

The day of Christ's death has become our true birthday. "Within the mystery of Christ dead and resurrected, death acquires positive value. Even if physical, biological death still appears to reign, it is no longer the final stage in a long destructive process. It has become the indispensable doorway, as well as the sure sign of our ultimate Pascha, our passage from death to life, rather than from life to death."[130]

From the beginning the Church observed an annual commemoration of the decisive and crucial three days of sacred history,
i.e., Great Friday, Great Saturday and Pascha. Great Friday and
Saturday have been observed as days of deep sorrow and strict
fast from Christian antiquity.

Great Friday and Saturday direct our attention to the trial,
crucifixion, death and burial of Christ. We are placed within the
awesome mystery of the extreme humility of our suffering God.
Therefore, these days are at once days of deep gloom as well as
watchful expectation. The Author of life is at work transforming
death into life: "Come, let us see our Life lying in the tomb, that
he may give life to those that in their tombs lie dead" (Sticheron
of Great Saturday Orthros).

Liturgically, the profound and awesome event of the death and
burial of God in the flesh is marked by a particular kind of silence,
i.e. by the absence of a eucharistic celebration. Great Friday and
Great Saturday are the only two days of the year when no
eucharistic assembly is held. However, before the twelfth century
it was the custom to celebrate the Liturgy of the Pre-Sanctified
Gifts on Great Friday.[131]

The focus of Great Friday is on the passion, death and burial
of our Lord Jesus Christ. The commentary (ὑπόμνημα) in the Triodion records it thusly: "On the Great and Holy Friday we commemorate the holy, saving and awesome sufferings of our Lord
and God and Saviour Jesus Christ: the spitting, the striking, the
scourging, the cursing, the mockery; the crown of thorns, the purple
cloak, the rod, the sponge, the vinegar and gall, the nails, the spear;
and above all the cross and the death, which He voluntarily endured for us. Also we commemorate the saving confession of the
grateful thief who was crucified with Him." Because of this emphasis on the passion of the Lord, the service of the Orthros of
Great Friday is often referred to in the liturgical books as the Service of the Holy Sufferings or Passion — Ἡ Ἀκολουθία τῶν Ἁγίων
Παθῶν. The hymns of this particular service are especially inspiring, rich and powerful.

The divine services of Great Friday with the richness of their
ample Scripture lessons, superb hymnography and vivid liturgical

actions bring the passion of Christ and its cosmic significance into sharp focus. The following hymns from the Orthros, Hours and Vespers help us to see how the Church understands and celebrates the awesome mystery of Christ's passion and death.

Today He who hung the earth upon the waters is hung upon the Cross. He who is King of the angels is arrayed in a crown of thorns. He who wraps the heavens in clouds is wrapped in the purple of mockery. He who in Jordan set Adam free receives blows upon His face. The Bridegroom of the Church is transfixed with nails. The Son of the Virgin is pierced with a spear. We venerate Thy Passion, O Christ. Show us also Thy glorious Resurrection.

(Fifteenth Antiphon)

When the transgressors nailed Thee, O Lord of glory, to the Cross, Thou hast cried aloud to them: 'How have I grieved you? Or wherein have I angered you? Before me, who delivered you from tribulation? And how do ye now repay me? Ye have given me evil for good: in return for the pillar of fire, ye have nailed me to the Cross; in return for the cloud, ye have dug a grave for me. Instead of manna, ye have given me gall; instead of water, ye have given me vinegar to drink. Henceforth I shall call the Gentiles, and they shall glorify me with the Father and the Holy Spirit.

(Ninth Hour)

A dread and marvelous mystery we see come to pass this day. He whom none may touch is seized; He who looses Adam from the curse is bound. He who tries the hearts and inner thoughts of man is unjustly brought to trial. He who closed the abyss is shut in prison. He before whom the powers of heaven stand with trembling, stands before Pilate; the Creator is struck by the hand of His creature. He who comes to judge the living and the dead is condemned to the Cross; the Destroyer of hell is enclosed in a tomb. O Thou who dost endure all these things in Thy tender love, who hast saved all men from the curse, O long-suffering Lord, glory to Thee.

(Sticheron of Vespers)

In the flesh Thou wast of Thine own will enclosed within

the tomb, yet in Thy divine nature Thou dost remain uncircumscribed and limitless. Thou hast shut up the treasury of hell, O Christ, and emptied all his palaces. Thou hast honored this Sabbath with Thy divine blessing, with Thy glory and Thy radiance.

(Apostichon of Vespers)

GENERAL OBSERVATIONS

In modern liturgical practice the Church celebrates three divine services on Great Friday: the Orthros, the Great Hours and the Great Vespers.

The Orthros of Great Friday

For the reasons we have already mentioned above, the Orthros of Great Friday is celebrated in anticipation on the evening of Great Thursday.

This service is the longest of all the divine services currently in use by the Church. Structurally, it is a modified fast day orthros with several distinctive and unique features which give it its own special identity and character.[132]

The first outstanding and unique feature of this service is that it contains a series of twelve Passion readings.[133] Because of this, the Orthros is known in popular piety as the Service of the Twelve Gospels (Ἀκολουθία τῶν Δώδεκα Εὐαγγελίων). The twelve pericopes are read at various intervals throughout the lengthy service. The first pericope, from the Gospel of John (13.21-18.1), relates the account of the Lord's discourse with the disciples at the Mystical Supper. The next ten pericopes deal with accounts of the Lord's sufferings as they are told in the Gospels.[134] The last pericope gives an account of the Lord's burial and the sealing of the Tomb. The response after each lection is a variation of the usual one: "Δόξα τῇ μακροθυμίᾳ σου, Κύριε, δόξα σοι — Glory to Your long-suffering, Lord, Glory to You." The focus of our praise is the forbearance of our God. This distinct liturgical formula signifies the deep reverence with which we approach the awesomeness of the divine condescension.

Another striking feature of this service is the solemn procession with the large Cross of the sanctuary, known in the liturgical language as the Ἐσταυρωμένος — The Crucified One.[135] After the fifth Gospel, at the fifteenth antiphon, the priest brings the Cross out of the sanctuary in a solemn procession and places it in the middle of the Church. This rite is relatively new. It originated in the Church of Antioch and was introduced into the Church of Constantinople in the year 1864 during the patriarchal reign of Sophronios. From there it found its way to all Greek-speaking churches.[136] The practice was authenticated and formalized by its inclusion in the Typicon of 1888. The rite is rooted in an ancient liturgical practice of the Church of Jerusalem. We are told by documents of the late fourth century that it was the custom in Jerusalem to display the relic of the true Cross at the Church of the Anastasis on Great Friday.[137] The procession of the Cross has become the focal point of the service. Hence in popular language the service is often referred to as the Service of the Crucified-One — Ἡ Ἀκολουθία τοῦ Ἐσταυρωμένου. More will be said about the procession below.

Another characteristic of this Orthros Service is the inclusion of a group of fifteen antiphons,[138] i.e. a set of hymns that were once used as responses to a corresponding number of Psalms. The Psalms have long since been suppressed. Only the troparia of the antiphons have remained in use. The most celebrated hymn of the Orthros service is the hymn of the fifteenth antiphon, "Σήμερον κρεμᾶται ἐπὶ ξύλου . . . — Today He who hung the earth upon the waters is hung upon the Tree (Cross) . . ."

Still another feature of this service is the inclusion of the Beatitudes (Μακαρισμοί).[139] They are chanted after the sixth Gospel. Hymns are interpolated between the verses of the Beatitudes.

The Great Hours (Αἰ Μεγάλαι Ὧραι)

In addition to the Vespers and the Orthros, the daily cycle of worship contains the Apodeipnon (Compline), the Midnight Service (Μεσονυκτικόν) and the Service of the Hours. These latter services have their roots in the devotional practices of the early Christians, and especially in the communal worship of the monastic communities.

Each of the four Hours bears a numerical name, derived from one of the major daylight hours or intervals of the day as they were known in antiquity: the First — Πρώτη — (corresponding to our sunrise); the Third — Τρίτη — (our midmorning or 9 a.m.); the Sixth — Ἔκτη — (our noonday); and the Ninth —Ἐνάτη — (our midafternoon or 3 p.m.).

Each Hour has a particular theme, and sometimes even a sub-theme, based upon some aspects of the Christ-event and salvation history. The general themes of the Hours are: the coming of Christ, the true light (First); the descent of the Holy Spirit (Third); the passion and crucifixion of Christ (Sixth); the death and burial of Christ (Ninth).

The central prayer of each Hour is the Lord's Prayer. In addition, each Hour has a set of three Psalms, hymns, a common prayer (Ὁ ἐν παντὶ καιρῷ), and a distinctive prayer for the Hour.

Slight variations occur in the Service of the Hours on feast days as well as on fast days. For example, in the place of the regular troparia, the apolytikia of the feast are read; or in the case of the Great Fast, penitial prayers are added at the end.

A radical change in the Service of the Hours, however, occurs on Great Friday. The content is altered and expanded with a set of troparia[140] and Scripture Readings (Prophecy, Epistle, and Gospel)[141] for each Hour. In addition, two of the three Psalms in each of the Hours are replaced with Psalms that reflect themes of Great Friday. While the stable-fixed Psalm of the service reflects the theme of the particular Hour, the variable Psalms reflect the theme of the day. In their expanded version these Hours are called The Great Hours. They are also known as the Royal Hours.[142] The services of the regular Hours are found in the Horologion. The Service of the Great Hours of Great Friday, however, is found in the Triodion.[143]

Originally each Hour was read at the appropriate time of the day. In a second stage of development, the first Hour was attached to the Orthros,[144] the Third and Sixth were read together in the late morning, and the Ninth preceded the Vespers. In a later development, the four Hours of Great Friday were grouped together and read in succession on the morning of Great Friday as a single office.

The Great Vespers

On the afternoon of Great Friday, we conduct the service of the Great Vespers with great solemnity.[145] This Vesper service concludes the remembrance of the events of the Lord's passion, and leads us towards watchful expectation as we contemplate the mystery of the Lord's descent into Hades, the theme of Great Saturday.

In popular language the Vesper Service of Great Friday is often called the Apokathelosis, a name derived from the liturgical re-enactment of the deposition of Christ from the Cross. The service is characterized by two dramatic liturgical actions: The *Deposition* or *Apokathelosis* ('Αποκαθήλωσις — literally the Un-nailing); and the *Procession of the Epitaphios* ('Επιτάφιος, i.e. the icon depicting the burial of Christ encased within a large embroidered cloth).

The rite of the Apokathelosis originated in the Church of Antioch. During the course of the nineteenth century it came to Constantinople and from there it passed gradually into the Church of Greece. At Constantinople it received the form we know and practice today.

Prior to the introduction of the solemn procession of the Estavromenos at the Orthros and the rite of the Apokathelosis at the Vespers, the churches practiced two simpler rituals. First, at the fifteenth antiphon of the Orthros, an icon of the crucifixion was brought in procession to the proskynetarion which stood in the middle of the solea. Second, at the Vesper service the Epitaphios was carried in solemn procession to the kouvouklion.[146]

In the Church of Antioch these two rituals developed along different lines. First, instead of an icon a large cross was carried in the procession at the Orthros. Fastened to the cross was a movable figure of the crucified Christ. Second, at the Vesper service the Epitaphios was carried in procession at the appointed time and was placed in the kouvouklion. Then, the figure of the crucified Christ was removed from the cross and placed in the kouvouklion. The figure was covered with a cloth and flowers. Last, the Gospel was placed in the kouvouklion.

These rites received a new form as they passed into the Greek Church. The rite of the Apokathelosis was lifted up and especially accentuated by attaching it to the reading of the Gospel at the Vesper service. As the priest intoned the passages of the lesson that narrate the event of the Deposition, the deacon re-enacted the Un-nailing. The figure of the Crucified Christ was removed from the Cross and wrapped in a new linen cloth. The figure was received by the priest, brought into the sanctuary and laid upon the Holy Table. After this the priest concluded the Gospel lesson. This dramatic representation of the Deposition has become the prevailing practice in the Greek Church.[147]

The procession with the Epitaphios is the second significant liturgical act of this service. It appears that the rite developed around the fifteenth century.[148] In some descriptions of the ritual, the procession takes place at the aposticha, while in others it takes place at the apolytikia. According to the order in the Patriarchal Text, the procession of the Epitaphios takes place at the aposticha.

Most descriptions of the procession presuppose a presence of several clerics. Let us look at one such description.[149] The Epitaphios is censed by the senior priest. It is then lifted up by four other priests who carry it above the head of the senior priest. He holds the Gospel Book (Εὐαγγέλιον). The deacon(s) precede(s) holding the censer.[150] However, it is obvious that such an elaborate ritual cannot be performed by only one priest, as is the case in most of our parishes today. For this reason, the ritual has been simplified in the current liturgical practice. Where two clergymen are present, both carry the Epitaphios. The senior priest precedes holding the Gospel in one hand and the Epitaphios over his head in the other. The second priest or deacon holds the other end of the Epitaphios over his head. If there is only one priest, he carries one end of the Epitaphios upon his head and holds the Gospel in the other hand. Two acolytes walk in back of him holding the other end of the Epitaphios. It is proper also for the Epitaphios to be held by four acolytes above the head of the priest. However, this is a rare occurrence in current usage. In some local traditions the Epitaphios is lifted up on poles, in order to facilitate the procedure. The Epitaphios is held high, above the head as a sign of deep reverence.[151]

The Gospel — It is important at this point to say something about the way the Gospel (Εὐαγγέλιον) is held at the processions of the Epitaphios on Great Friday. In the liturgical tradition of our Church, the Gospel is considered to be the chief icon of Christ. Therefore, as the rituals of the passion began to develop, the Gospel Book was given special attention by the way it was held and adorned. Long before the Epitaphios was introduced into the liturgy of Great Friday, it was the Gospel, wrapped in the aer, that was carried in the processions. The aer symbolized the burial cloth. To further depict the death of Christ, the Gospel was held flat upon the right shoulder of the celebrant, instead of the usual upright position.

The Icon — On Great Friday besides the Cross and the Epitaphios we display the icon known as the ""Ἄχρα Ταπείνωσις — The Extreme Humility." This icon depicts the crucified dead body of Christ upright in the Tomb with the Cross in the background. It combines the two awesome events of Great Friday, the crucifixion and burial of Christ.

Fasting — Great Friday is a day of strict fast, a day of xerophagia.

Liturgical Preparations — In advance of the service, the priest has made certain that: the Epitaphios is prepared; the Kouvouklion is decorated; there are ample flowers for distribution to the faithful; and a new white linen cloth is purchased to be used at the Apokathelosis. He also prepares a tray of rose petals and the ραντιστήριον (sprinkler) containing rose-water or another fragrant water, that will be used after the procession of the Epitaphios.

The Estavromenos — The Cross, placed in the middle of the solea at the Orthros, remains there throughout the services of Great Friday. However, in order to make room for the Kouvouklion it should be moved closer to the sanctuary steps before the service of the Vespers. At the conclusion of the service of the Orthros of Great Saturday, the Cross is returned to its usual place in the sanctuary. By custom, the crown of flowers remains on the Cross until the Apodosis of Pascha. The candles, however, are removed. *The Kouvouklion* is decorated before the Vesper service. After the reading of the Gospel and prior to the procession of the Epitaphios, it is moved to the middle of the solea in front of the Cross. The Cross and Kouvouklion are placed in front of the Holy Doors in the middle of the solea.

The distribution of flowers — In current practice the flowers are usually distributed at the conclusion of the Orthros of Great Saturday. However, in some parishes it has become the custom to distribute flowers at the conclusion of the Vespers of Great Friday as well, especially to children who may not be in attendance at the later service.

RUBRICS

The Orthros

According to the current liturgical practice, the Orthros of Great Friday is celebrated on the evening of Great Thursday. Because this service is complex and filled with musical variations, special care should be taken to execute the hymns well.

The vestments — The priest wears a black or deep purple epitrachilion and phelonion. The holy Table is dressed with a black or purple cloth.

The Cross — It is customary to place a crown of flowers of adequate, moderate proportions upon the large Cross of the sanctuary. Also, three candles are placed on the bars of the Cross, one on the verticle bar and two on either end of the horizontal bar.[152] These preparations are made in advance of the service.

The priest censes with the katzion during the intonation of the Royal Psalms at the beginning of the service.

The Order of the Service — The service is conducted in accordance with the order and the rubrics of the Patriarchal Text. Between the sets of hymns the priest intones the prescribed lections, litanies and prayers.

The Gospel lessons — According to current practice the priest reads the Gospels from the Holy Gate. By custom, the 12th Gospel is read from the amvon (pulpit).

The Procession — By custom, the Holy Gate is closed after the 5th

Gospel. The priest prepares for the procession of the Cross. The
Cross is brought to the Holy Table and is censed. When the time
comes for the "Σήμερον κρεμᾶται ἐπὶ ξύλου . . . — Today He Who
hung the earth . . ." (15th Antiphon) — the priest lifts up the Cross.
He carries it as if he would carry an icon in procession, and intones simply and clearly the troparion "Σήμερον κρεμᾶται." The
acolytes and chanters go before him. The procession proceeds
through the north door of the sanctuary (by the Prothesis) and
up the north aisle, around and down the south aisle of the Church
to the solea, where a stand has been placed to receive the Cross.
The priest reverently places the Cross in the stand. The chanters
then sing the troparion "Σήμερον κρεμᾶται." By custom, the priest
and the congregation kneel until the troparion is completed. The
priest then venerates the Estavromenos and returns to the sanctuary to resume the readings at the appointed times.

It should be noted that the Estavromenos remains in place
on the solea throughout all of the services on Great Friday.
The Apolysis has its own particular prologue. "'Ο ἐμπτυσμοὺς καὶ
μάστιγας . . . — May He Who endured spitting and scourging . . ."
Veneration of the Cross — The congregation venerates the
Estavromenos in accordance with local custom. Care should be
taken to protect the solemnity of the service. In most places the
congregation reverences the Estavromenos at the conclusion of
the service.

The Great Hours

The Great Hours are chanted and read as one service on Great
Friday morning, in accordance with the order found in the Patriarchal Text.

The priest wears the epitrachelion and phelonion, as in the
preceding Orthros service.

The four Gospel lessons, one for each of the Hours, are read
from the Holy Doors.

The priest censes the sanctuary, the church and the people
in the usual manner with the katzion, while the troparia are being chanted at the Third Hour. He may choose to repeat the censing at the Sixth and Ninth Hours.

At the Ninth Hour the hymn "Σήμερον κρεμᾶται" is intoned by the reader or chanter. By custom the reader stands before the Cross when intoning the hymn. When he has completed the hymn, it is chanted by the choirs.

The Apolysis is the same as at the preceding Orthros.

The Vespers
The Order — The Vespers of Great Friday are patterned after the festal Great Vesper service. This will be the first time during the course of Great Week that we use the order of a festive service in the Daily Office. This is significant in as much as it signals the beginning of the transformation of λύπη (sorrow) into χαρά (joy).

The service is conducted in the usual manner and order. The litanies and prayers said by the priest are found in the Ἱερατικόν under the rubric of the Great Vespers. The hymns are chanted in the order that appears in the Patriarchal Text.

The Entrance — The Entrance (Εἴσοδος) is made with the Gospel, which is held in the usual upright position.

The Lessons — The Prokeimena and Scripture Lessons follow. The Readings consist of three Old Testament pericopes, an Epistle lesson, and a long Gospel pericope.[153]

The Apokathelosis — The Apokathelosis takes place during the concluding verses of the Gospel lesson, or at the conclusion of the lesson. The priest comes before the Cross; censes the Estavromenos; removes the figure from the Cross; wraps it in the linen cloth; and brings it into the sanctuary and places it upon the Holy Table.[154]

The Litanies and Prayers — The Fervent Litany, the "Evening Prayer," the Petitions, Peace, and Prayer for the bowing of the head, follow.

The Epitaphios — At the aposticha, we conduct the procession of the Epitaphios. The Epitaphios is placed on the Holy Table before the enarxis of the Vespers or after the reading of the Gospel. Before lifting it for the procession the priest censes the Epitaphios. The procession forms[155] and proceeds through the north door of the sanctuary. As in other solemn processions, the Epitaphios is carried up the north aisle, around the Church and down the south aisle. It is brought to the Kouvouklion,[156] which has been placed in the middle of the solea, and deposited in it. The priest then moves around the Kouvouklion censing the Epitaphios from each of the four sides. By custom, he also sprinkles the Epitaphios with rose-water and scatters rose-petals and flowers on it. The priest then places the Gospel (Εὐαγγέλιον) upon the Epitaphios. After the Apolysis the priest and the faithful venerate the Epitaphios.

The Apolysis — After the "δόξα καὶ νῦν" of the aposticha, we intone the hymn of St. Symeon as usual. The Trisagion prayers, the apolytikia, and the apolysis follow.

Note — The divine services of Great Friday conclude with the Vespers. However, in the evening of Great Friday we celebrate the Orthros of Great Saturday by anticipation.

Chapter Five

The Great and Holy Saturday

COMMENTS ON THE MAIN THEMES

On Great Saturday the Church contemplates the mystery of the Lord's descent into Hades, the place of the dead. Death, our ultimate enemy, is defeated from within. "He (Christ) gave Himself as a ransom to death in which we were held captive, sold under sin. Descending into Hades through the Cross . . . He loosed the bonds of death" (Liturgy of St. Basil). The hymnographer of the Church describes the mystery with these words:

Come, let us see our Life lying in the tomb, that He may give life to those that in their tombs lie dead. Come, let us look today on the Son of Judah as He sleeps, and with the prophet let us cry aloud to Him: Thou hast lain down, Thou hast slept as a lion; who shall awaken Thee, O King? But of Thine own free will do Thou rise up, who willingly dost give Thyself for us. O Lord, glory to Thee.

Today a tomb holds Him who holds the creation in the hollow of His hand; a stone covers Him who covered the heavens with glory. Life sleeps and hell trembles, and Adam is set free from his bonds. Glory to Thy dispensation, whereby Thou hast accomplished all things, granting us an eternal Sabbath, Thy most holy Resurrection from the dead.

(*Hymns of the Ainoi*)

On Great Saturday our focus is on the Tomb of Christ. This is no ordinary grave. It is not a place of corruption, decay and defeat. It is life-giving (ζωοποιός) a source of power, victory and liberation.

O happy tomb! It received within itself the Creator, as one asleep, and it was made a divine treasury of life, for our salvation who sing: O God our Deliverer, blessed art Thou.

77

The Life of all submits to be laid in the tomb, according to the
law of the dead, and He makes it a source of awakening, for our
salvation who sing: O God our Deliverer, blessed art Thou.

(*Hymns of the 7th Ode*)

Great Saturday is the day between Jesus' death and His resurrection. It is the day of watchful expectation, in which mourning
is being transformed into joy. The day embodies in the fullest possible sense the meaning of χαρμολύπη — joyful-sadness, which has
dominated the celebrations of Great Week. The hymnographer
of the Church has penetrated the profound mystery, and helps
us to understand it through the following poetic dialogue that he
has devised between Jesus and His Mother:

Weep not for me, O Mother, beholding in the sepulcher the Son
whom thou hast conceived without seed in thy womb. For I shall
rise and shall be glorified, and as God I shall exalt in everlasting
glory those who magnify thee with faith and love.

"O Son without beginning, in ways surpassing nature was I blessed
at Thy strange birth, for I was spared all travail. But now
beholding Thee, my God, a lifeless corpse, I am pierced by the
sword of bitter sorrow. But arise, that I may be magnified."

"By mine own will the earth covers me, O Mother, but the
gatekeepers of hell tremble as they see me, clothed in the blood-
stained garment of vengeance: for on the Cross as God have I
struck down mine enemies, and I shall rise again and magnify
thee."

"Let the creation rejoice exceedingly, let all those born on earth
be glad: for hell, the enemy, has been despoiled. Ye women, come
to meet me with sweet spices: for I am delivering Adam and Eve
with all their offspring, and on the third day I shall rise again."

(*9th Ode of the Canon*)

Great Saturday is the day of the pre-eminent rest. Christ
observes a Sabbath rest in the tomb. His rest, however, is not inactivity but the fulfillment of the divine will and plan for the salvation of humankind and the cosmos. He who brought all things

into being, makes all things new. The recreation of the world has been accomplished once and for all. Through His incarnation, life and death Christ has filled all things with Himself. He has opened a path for all flesh to the resurrection from the dead, since it was not possible that the author of life would be dominated by corruption.[157]

> Moses the great mystically prefigured this present day, saying: "And God blessed the seventh day." For this is the blessed Sabbath, this is the day of rest, on which the only-begotten Son of God rested from all His works. Suffering death in accordance with the plan of salvation, He kept the Sabbath in the flesh; and returning once again to what He was, through His Resurrection He has granted us eternal life, for He alone is good and loves mankind.
>
> *(Hymn of the Ainoi)*

St. Paul tells us that "God was in Jesus Christ reconciling the world to Himself" (2 Cor 5.19). Hence, eternal life — real and self-generating — penetrated the depths of Hades. Christ who is the life of all destroyed death by His death. That is why the Church sings joyously "Things now are filled with light, the heaven and the earth and all that is beneath the earth" (Canon of Pascha). The Church knows herself to be "the place, the eternal reality, where the presence of Christ vanquishes Satan, hell and death itself."[158]

The solemn observance of Great Saturday help us to recall and celebrate the great truth that "despite the daily vicissitudes and contradictions of history and the abiding presence of hell within the human heart and human society,"[159] life has been liberated! Christ has broken the power of death.

The death of Christ is the greatest miracle as well as the ultimate manifestation of God's boundless love for the whole creation. It is no mere man who died. The One who was laid in the tomb is none other than the eternal and deathless Word of God, who taking on flesh humbled Himself, obediently accepting even death, death on a cross (Phil 2.8). Pascha has nothing to do with romanticism and sentimentalities. Someone put it in these bold, vivid terms: "Easter is not about the return of the robin in spring or crocuses or a butterfly coming out of the cocoon or any of that pagan drivel. Its about a Body that somehow got loose. The Gospel accounts strain to describe what happened, but don't make any mistake about it, they're trying to describe something unearthly: death working backwards. So I can't talk about 'the eternal rebirth of hope' or 'Jesus living on in our hearts.' We're talking about a dead Jew, crucified, who came back to life . . . This is God we're talking about, a real God, people, not some projection of our ego."

It is not without significance that the icon of the Resurrection in our Church is the Descent of Christ into Hades, the place of the dead. This icon depicts a victorious Christ, reigned in glory, trampling upon death, and seizing Adam and Eve in His hands, plucking them from the abyss of hell. This icon expresses vividly the truths resulting from Christ's defeat of death by His death and resurrection.

GENERAL OBSERVATIONS

Divine Services

The observances of Great Saturday include the whole cycle of the daily office. In practice, however, only the Vespers and the Orthros are celebrated in the parishes. The Vespers are part of the Great Friday afternoon celebration, as noted above.

The Orthros, for the reasons we have mentioned above, is celebrated on the evening of Great Friday.[160]

This is the only day in the entire liturgical year, for which the Church may not assemble for a eucharistic celebration. Sadly, however, this prohibition has been inadvertently circumvented by a faulty liturgical practice, caused by the gradual transfer of the Paschal Vesperal Liturgy to the morning hours of Great Saturday.

Vestments — The priest begins the service wearing the rason and a black or purple colored epitrachelion. When the chanters or choir begin the fourth ode of the Canon, the priest retires to the vestry. There he vests, putting on a full set of his priestly vestments.[161] This time the priest wears bright colored vestments, because of the transitional character of the service.

The Fast — In the tradition of our Church, Saturday like Sunday is considered a festal day. Even during the Great Lent the rules of fasting are relaxed on Saturdays and Sundays. However, Great Saturday is the one important exception. The day is observed with xerophagia. The fast is so strict that Great Saturday is observed with profound silence. I mean by this, that the Divine Liturgy is not celebrated.

Candles — It is customary for the clergy and people to hold candles during the singing of the Lamentations and at the procession of the Epitaphios. It is necessary, therefore, to make certain that a sufficient number of candles have been prepared and distributed to the faithful. This practice is rooted in ancient Christian burial practices. Candles were lit in order to symbolize the victory of Christ over death, and to express as well the Church's belief in the resurrection.

The Ἐγκώμια — Encomia

The Encomia[162] or Praises are short poetic verses lamenting the passion, death and burial of Christ. The Encomia are also known as Ἐπιτάφιος θρῆνος'' — Lamentations and more rarely Ἐπιτάφια Μεγαλυνάρια — Burial Megalynaria.[163]

In the printed Triodia, as well as the 1906 edition of the Patriarchal Text, there are 185 such verses divided into three staseis (sections). The repertoire of the Encomia first appeared in the 1522 edition of the Triodion. Subsequent editions have relied heavily on this source.

The early manuscripts do not mention these hymns. The first reference to encomia is found in manuscripts of the thirteenth century in connection with Psalm 118 (119), known as the Ἄμωμος — Amomos.[164] Their number, however, is undefined. It appears that the collection grew gradually to its present form.[165] Also, there are variations in the collections.[166]

The Amomos[167] is the longest of the Old Testament Psalms, containing one hundred seventy six verses. It plays an important role in the liturgical tradition of the Orthodox Church. Divided into three sections, it comprises the entire Seventeenth Kathisma of the Psalter. The Amomos forms part of the Saturday and Sunday Orthros.[168] On Sundays the Amomos is read as the third

Kathisma, while on Saturday it is always read as the second Kathisma. The first, second and third Kathisma always precede the Canon in the order of the Orthros. Thus, in all the editions of the Triodion the Encomia appear before the Canon in the order of the Orthros of Great Saturday. However, the same is not true for the Patriarchal Text of Great Week. There, the Encomia appear after the Canon.

This discrepancy between the Triodion and the prevailing practice of the Greek Church regarding the place of the Encomia in the order of the service is difficult to explain. I suspect that some practical considerations prompted the change. As late as the turn of this century, the time for the celebration of the Great Saturday Orthros had not yet been definitively settled. Some places continued to celebrate the service after midnight in the early morning hours of Great Saturday, while most other places had already shifted the service to the evening of Great Friday.[169] In either case, the change in the order of the service allowed more time for the faithful to assemble and participate in this highly popular part of the service.[170]

It is not clear when the change in the order had begun. We do know that it was authenticated, confirmed and formalized by the new Typika in the last century.

The Encomia are interpolated short refrains of lamentation added to the Amomos. The division of the Encomia into three staseis corresponds to the Amomos, which, as we have already noted, is divided into three sections and forms the Seventeenth Kathisma of the Psalter. The Encomia were sung after each verse of the Psalter. This arrangement continues to be observed in monasteries. For the most part, however, in parish usage — at least in the Greek liturgical practice — the Amomos has long since been suppressed. Only the Encomia are sung in three staseis.[171]

The full repertoire[172] of the Encomia are no longer said in parish usage. The tendency to decrease the number of verses has always been operative for a variety of reasons.[173] In recent times several such smaller collections have appeared in print. For example, the first eight editions of the Patriarchal Text printed by the Apostolike Diakonia contained only thirty verses for each

stasis.[174] To my knowledge the shortest collection is contained in
the Greek-English Services For Holy Week and Easter Sunday,
published in London in 1915.[175] In our own country, the number
of verses varies from parish to parish. In most places, however,
the collection has been determined more or less by the following
three editions: (1) The earlier editions of the Patriarchal Text by
the Apostolike Diakonia; (2) the *Holy Week — Easter*, edited by
Fr. George Papadeas;[176] and (3) the O Logos *Good Friday Evening — The Service of the Lamentations, edited by Fr. George
Mastrantonis.*[177]

The Evlogetaria — are the Καθίσματα τροπάρια — sessional hymns
of the Amomos.[178]

In our liturgical tradition there are two types of Evlogetaria,
the resurrectional and funereal. The resurrectional Evlogetaria
are sung on Sundays.[179] The funereal are always chanted on
Saturdays and at funeral services.[180]

On Great Saturday, however, we sing the resurrectional
Evlogetaria and not the funereal, even though we are observing
the burial of Christ. The reason for this is clear. On Great Saturday we contemplate the defeat of death. The Author of life is trampling down Hades and is transforming death into life. Funereal hymns
are not appropriate to Him Who is the source and giver of all life.
Also, the funeral evlogetaria as written would be inappropriate for
Christ, since they presuppose deceased Christians.[181]

RUBRICS

The Orthros of Great Saturday is festive in nature, with the
"Θεὸς Κύριος" — God is the Lord" at the beginning, and a sung
Great Doxology at the end. The service contains several distinctive features. The order of the service is as follows:
The Enarxis to Psalm 50 — The service is conducted in the usual
manner from the Enarxis to the Kathismata and the recitation
of Psalm 50. The order is articulated clearly in the Patriarchal Text.

The Canon[182]

The choirs begin the Canon after the Reader has completed
the recitation of Psalm 50. The Holy Door, according to custom,

is closed when the Canon begins.

The Canon is chanted in the prescribed manner. At the appointed intervals the priest intones the Small Litany.

When the Eighth Ode has been sung, the priest, as usual, intones the bidding "Τὴν Θεοτόκον καὶ Μητέρα τοῦ Φωτός — Let us magnify the Theotokos." However, he does not offer the incense.

The choir sings the Ninth Ode of the Canon. When the Canon is concluded the Holy Doors are opened. The priest stands before the Holy Table holding a candle and the θυμιατόν (thurible —censer).

The choir and chanters along with the acolytes proceed to the Epitaphios and stand on either side. The candles of the Kouvouklion are lit.

The Encomia — Ἐγκώμια

The Encomia are accompanied by two ritual acts. When the Canon has been completed, the Holy Doors are opened. The priest holds a candle and the thurible (censer). He chants the first verse of the First Stasis and proceeds to the Epitaphios. He censes the Kouvouklion cross-wise (i.e., on each side), the iconostasion and the people, in the usual manner at an Orthros service.

The priest stands in front of the Kouvouklion throughout the Encomia. Between each stasis of the Encomia the priest intones the Small Litany with the prescribed ecphonesis noted in the Patriarchal Text. At the Third Stasis when the verse "Ἔρραναν τὸν Τάφον αἱ μυροφόροι μύρα, λίαν πρωΐ ἐλθοῦσαι — Early in the morning the myrrh-bearers came to Thee and sprinkled myrrh upon Thy tomb" is sung the priest sprinkles the Epitaphios with rosewater, using the ραντιστήριον (sprinkler). This verse is usually repeated three or more times. It has become the custom to sprinkle the people as well.

When the Encomia have been completed the priest returns to the sanctuary. The acolytes, chanters and choir also return to their place.

The Evlogetaria — Εὐλογητάρια

When the Encomia have been concluded, the choir or chanters sing the Evlogetaria in a stately manner.

The Exaposteilarion, Ainoi and Doxology

Following the Evlogetaria the priest intones the Small Litany, after which we sing the Exaposteilarion. It consists only of the verse ""Ἅγιος Κύριος ὁ Θεὸς ἡμῶν — Holy is the Lord our God," as at the Orthros for Sundays. There are no Exaposteilarion hymns.

The psalms of Praise and the hymns are then chanted. They are followed by the Great Doxology at the end of which we conduct the procession of the Epitaphios.[183]

The Procession of the Epitaphios

The procession of the Epitaphios takes place at the conclusion of the Doxology. To be precise, the rubrics say that the procession begins when the choir sings the concluding segment of the Doxology, the ""Ἅγιος ὁ Θεός — Holy God."[184]

The procession is usually conducted around the outside of the Church.[185] According to custom the procession is formed in the following manner: first to proceed are the acolytes holding the processional cross, hexapteryga, candles and censer; the large Cross of the Estavromenos follows; then the priest, holding the Gospel in a raised but flat position;[186] the Epitaphios is carried last.[187] The people, holding candles follow the Epitaphios. In some places the clergy process in back of the Epitaphios at the head of the people. The former order, however, appears to be older and in keeping with tradition.[188]

In some traditions, it is the custom to make three or four staseis (stops) during the procession. At each staseis the priest intones petitions of the Fervent Litany.

During the procession the choir and people sing the ""Ἅγιος ὁ Θεός — Holy God" in a solemn manner.[189] In many places, however, it has become the practice to repeat some of the Encomia. This is clearly an innovation, and probably a concession to popular devotional piety.

The procession returns to the interior of the Church. In many places it is customary for the faithful to pass under the Epitaphios before reentering the Church. In this instance, the Epitaphios is held aloft, while the clergy and people pass under it. By this practice, we express the belief that we have already passed from death to life (Jn 5.24).

The Return of the Epitaphios to the Holy Table

When the procession has returned to the Church and everyone has taken their place, the priest says: "Πρόσχωμεν — Let us be attentive." He then gives the peace, "Εἰρήνη πᾶσι — Peace be with all." And says, "Σοφία — Wisdom."

After this the priest and the people sing the apolytikia of the Vesper service. In earlier times only the hymn "Noble Joseph" was sung at this point. Today, however, all three hymns are sung in the following order: "῞Οτε κατῆλθες," "Ταῖς Μυροφόροις γυναιξί" and "῾Ο εὐσχήμων ᾿Ιωσήφ — Noble Joseph."

While these hymns are being sung, the priest censes the Epitaphios. Then he lifts it out of the Kouvouklion and carries it into the sanctuary through the Holy Doors. He circles the Holy Table three times and places the Epitaphios upon it, when the words "ἐν μνήματι καινῷ κηδεύσας ἀπέθετο — and he laid it in a new tomb" — of the hymn Noble Joseph are being sung.[190] The Epitaphios remains on the Holy Table until the feast of the Apodosis of Pascha.[191]

The people venerate the Epitaphios at the Vesper service and upon entering the Church for the service of the Orthros on Great Friday evening. It is customary for the people to receive a flower. This is done in two ways. The flowers can be distributed at the end of the service, usually by the priest. This seems to be the prevailing practice in the Greek Orthodox Archdiocese. Or they can be distributed by some designated person(s) to the people after they have venerated the Epitaphios during the course of the service. In either case, care must be given to preserve the proper decorum and solemnity.

The Readings to the Apolysis

After the Epitaphios has been deposited upon the Holy Table, the choir sings the hymn of the Prophecy. Then, the Reader intones the Prokeimenon (Ps 43) and reads the Old Testament pericope (Ezekiel 37.1-14). The Prokeimenon (Ps 9) and Epistle reading (1 Cor 5.6-8; Gal 3.13-14) follow. When the Epistle lesson has been concluded, the priest gives the peace to the Reader; and the Prokeimenon (Ps 67) with the Alleluia is chanted. Then, the priest bids the people to listen to the Holy Gospel and gives the peace in the usual manner. The priest proceeds to the amvon, where, by custom, he intones the pericope of the Gospel (Mt 27.62-66).[192]

After the Readings, the priest intones the Dismissal Litany; gives the peace; and reads the prayer for the bowing of heads after the usual bidding.

The Apolysis is conducted in the usual manner. The prologue is peculiar to the day.

Since the office of the Hours has been omitted in parish usage,[193] the Orthros service concludes the solemnities of Great Saturday.[194] The Divine Liturgy which is now celebrated on Great Saturday morning properly belongs to the Paschal Vigil. Great Saturday is the only day of the year without a Divine Liturgy. While this is true also for Great Friday in current liturgical practice, at one time the Pre-sanctified Liturgy was celebrated on Great Friday.[195]

Chapter Six

The Great and Holy Pascha

COMMENTS ON THE MAIN THEMES

Great Week comes to an end at sunset of Great Saturday, as the Church prepares to celebrate her most ancient and preeminent festival, Pascha, the feast of feasts. The time of preparation will give way to the time of fulfillment. The glorious and resplendent light emanating from the Empty Tomb will dispel the darkness. Christ, risen from the dead, cracks the fortress of death and takes "captivity captive" (Ps 67.19). All the limitations of our createdness are torn asunder. Death is swallowed up in victory and life is liberated. "For as by a man came death, by a man came also the resurrection of the dead. For as in Adam all die, so also in Christ shall all be made alive" (1 Cor 15.21-22). Pascha is the dawn of the new and unending day. The resurrection constitutes the most radical and decisive deliverance of humankind.

The resurrection of Jesus Christ is the fundamental truth and absolute fact of the Christian faith. It is the central experience and essential kerygma of the Church. It confirms the authenticity of Christ's remarkable earthly life and vindicates the truth of His teaching. It seals all His redemptive work: His life, the model of a holy life; His compelling and unique teaching; His extraordinary works; and His awesome, life-creating death. Christ's resurrection is the guarantee of our salvation. Together with His ascension it brings to perfection God's union with us for all eternity.[196]

The resurrection made possible the miracle of the Church, which in every age and generation proclaims and affirms "God's plan for the universe, the ultimate divinization of man and the created order."[197] The profound experience of and the unshakable belief in the risen Lord enabled the Apostles to evangelize the world and empowered the Church to overcome paganism. The resurrection discloses the indestructible power and inscrutable wisdom of God. It disposes of the illusory myths and belief systems

89

by which people, bereft of divine knowledge, strain to affirm the meaning and purpose of their existence. Christ, risen and glorified, releases humanity from the delusions of idolatry. In Him grave-bound humanity discovers and is filled with incomparable hope. The resurrection bestows illumination, energizes souls, brings forgiveness, transfigures lives, creates saints, and gives joy.

The resurrection "introduced a definitive moment in human existence."[198] An historical person conquered death (1 Cor 15.21-22). The dynamic restoration of the fulness of human existence was accomplished once and for all.[199] St. John of Damascus says, "Although Christ died as a man and His holy soul was separated from His most pure body, His divinity remained both with the soul and the body, continued inseparably from either."[200] Developing this idea, Fr. Florovsky notes that Christ's death "was a death within the hypostasis of the Word, the death of the 'enhypostasized' humanity. Death in general is a separation, and in the death of the Lord His most precious body and soul were separated indeed. But the one hypostasis of the Word Incarnate was not divided, the 'hypostatic union' was not broken or destroyed. In other words, though separated in death, the soul and the body remained still united through the divinity of the Word, from which neither was estranged. This does not alter the ontological character of death, but changes its meaning. This was an incorrupt death."[201] The body of Christ did not suffer corruption as it happens with our bodies at death. His body never became a corpse.[202] Rather, corruption and death were overcome in it by virtue of the hypostatic union which is the source of the resurrection. Thus, the very death of the Incarnate reveals the resurrection of human nature.

The resurrection has not yet abolished the reality of death. But it has revealed its powerlessness (Heb 2.14-15). We continue to die, because we die out, as a result of the Fall. Our bodies decay and fall away. "God allows death to exist but turns it against corruption and its cause sin, and sets a boundary both to corruption and sin," writes Panayiotis Nellas.[203] Thus, physical death does not destroy our life of communion with God. Rather, we move from death to life; from this fallen world to God's reign.

Death disrupts and dissolves the fundamental unity of the human person, created by God as "a single psycho-physical organism made of two elements, soul and body."[204] Following the lead of the Greek Fathers, Father Clapsis names death as "the ultimate ontological distortion of man's nature."[205] According to Father Florovsky, "A dead man is not fully human. A body without a soul is but a corpse, and a soul without a body is a ghost. Man is not a ghost without a body, and a corpse is not a part of man . . . That is why the separation of soul and body is the death of man himself, the discontinuation of his existence, of his existence as a man. Consequently, death and the corruption of the body are a sort of falling away of the 'image of God' in man."[206] However, it is precisely here that we discover the meaning of Christ's resurrection as the abolishment of Hades and the reintegration of human nature.

Hades, "the place of hopeless disembodiment and disincarnation,"[207] has been annihilated by Christ's resurrection. In Christ "all human nature is fully and completely cured from unwholeness and mortality. This restoration will be actualized and revealed to its full extent in the general resurrection, in the resurrection of all."[208] Christ has healed our dreadful brokenness and tragic unfulfillment. "We are dissolved for a time only, according to our bodies' mortal nature; like seeds cast into the earth, we do not perish, but sown in the earth we shall rise again, death being brought to nought by the grace of the Savior," says St. Athanasios.[209] Every death, i.e., every separation of soul and body, every disembodiment is temporary, for all will rise. Therefore, dying is no longer a defeat. The death of the body becomes a sleep and death itself the gate of life. In Christ, the life of the flesh is being continuously transfigured into a life of the spirit; and this life knows no limits or decrease. The Holy Spirit sows the seed of immortality into our bodies and renews our souls daily (2 Cor 5.1-5).

The hymns of the feast abound with references to our deliverance from the destructive power of evil and death. The following sticheron is one such example:

Today Hades groans and cries aloud: "My dominion has been

swallowed up; the Shepherd has been crucified and He has raised Adam. I am deprived of those whom I once ruled; in my strength I devoured them, but now I have cast them forth. He who was crucified has emptied the tombs, the power of death has no more strength." Glory to thy Cross, O Lord, and to thy Resurrection.

(*Great Vespers of Pascha*)

Christ has become the Land of the Living ('H Χώρα τῶν Ζώντων) for those on either side of death who believe in His Name. The living and the dead "form one body, and through the same prayer are united into one before the throne of the Lord of glory. The experience of this unity through all times is revealed and sealed in the whole cycle of worship . . . Christ reigns equally in the Church — among the departed and among the living, for God is not the God of the dead but of the living."[210]

We share in and experience the resurrection of Christ in two ways. First, it is the source for the continual mystical and spiritual regeneration of our dead souls. Second, it is the cause of our resurrection from the dead on the Last Day.

Though the consequences of Christ's resurrection will be disclosed fully at the Parousia, participation in these eternal blessings begins here in this life. Christ, according to St. Symeon the New Theologian, "grants us the grace to have His kingdom within us, so that we will not remain merely in the hope of entering. We truly possess it as we cry out, 'our life is hidden with Christ in God.' "[211] He adds, "Let us carefully examine the mystery of the resurrection of Christ our God which takes place mystically at all times, if we desire it: how He is buried within us as in a tomb. He is joined to our souls and rises again, and He raises us up with Himself."[212] For those who live in faith and surrender themselves voluntarily to the will and love of God, the resurrection becomes a daily reality. Souls are quickened, sins are forgiven, the mind is illumined and the heart is purified, as the Holy Spirit forms the mind of Christ in us.

God wants to make us gods by grace, men that we are, but with our consent and not against our will," says St. Symeon.[213] The miracle of Pascha, with its promise and gift of eternity and plenitude, is always accessible to everyone. However, salvation is accomplished only in perfect freedom, through an act of faith. No one can be compelled to believe in or to love God. To receive the grace of the Paschal mystery and to keep it operative in us we must want to engage ourselves actively and creatively in the godly life by the power of the Holy Spirit. A note of caution, however, is required here. Salvation does not come about merely as a result of individualistic piety, but through a living and dynamic relationship with the Church. As baptized devout members of the Church we become part of a community which is moving together towards the Kingdom. It is this community which affirms and defines our Christian identity. In and through the Church we appropriate the transforming power of the death and resurrection of Christ, which places upon us the obligation to actualize the renunciations demanded of us by the Gospel in our everyday activities. The faith community reminds us continuously of our vocation and helps us to realize our ultimate destiny. It calls us to abjure the false values of the fallen world and inspires us to seek after all that is noble, good, natural, and sinless. It encourages us to struggle against all forms of oppression and unjust conditions which devalue and diminish human life; do more for the life of others in the world; and work for the fulfillment of the Church's vocation in the world.

The fruits of Christ's saving death and resurrection are granted to us and are accomplished especially through the sacraments celebrated in faith. Through them the new life is extended and given to the members of His body, the Church. The sacraments prepare the faithful for the resurrectional life and simultaneously make that life a living reality in this present age. Through them Christ calls us to share intimately in what is divine: immortality (ἀθανασία) and incorruptibility (ἀφθαρσία).[214] He sends and grants us the Holy Spirit, who continually vivifies our souls and actualizes within us the hidden mysteries of God's kingdom, joining us to God in a personal union.

Christ who exalted our flesh by assuming our humanity will raise our bodies from the dead at the Last Day (Jn 5.28-29). The resurrection of the dead is inevitable. "It does not depend upon our will, whether we rise after death or not, just as it is not by our will that we are born." Everyone, believers and non-believers alike, "will recover their bodies and enter into everlasting life, if essentially differing a life," writes Georgios Mantzarides.[215] "No one, so far as nature is concerned, can escape Christ's kingly rule, can alienate himself from the power of the resurrection," notes Fr. Florovsky.[216] The resurrection of the dead on the Last Day is the common destiny of all, " because we all have the same nature as the Man Christ Jesus,"[217] whose death and resurrection brings immortality and incorruption to all. Only sinners will be surprised by it. The final day will appear suddenly and Christ will shine in everyone. His light will be the ineffable joy and blessedness of the righteous, but a burning and consuming fire of judgment for the unjust. "The day of the Lord is not for those who are constantly illumined by the divine light. It is for those who live in the darkness of passion and who spend their days in this world desiring the (sinful) things of the world," observes St. Symeon the New Theologian.[218] He adds, "those who will have become children of this light and sons of the day to come . . . will never know the Day of the Lord, for they are in it unceasingly. (But) for those who live in darkness the day will be suddenly revealed: for them it will be frightening, like unbearable fire."[219]

All who willfully ignore and reject God and despise His commandments in this life, will continue to cling to their selfishness in the age to come. Therefore, they will experience the resurrection as judgment and hell.

Hell is found on either side of death. It is not a place, but a state of being, a state of radical unfulfillment, an act of apostasy, a severance of the ultimate relationship, a deliberate rejection of God. Fr. Florovsky describes it as "a state of personal disintegration, which is mistaken for self-assertion; a state of self-confinement, of isolation and alienation, of proud solitude."[220] God does not send anyone to hell. Hell is made by the devil and by men, who persist in their rebellion against God, His truth and love.

The resurrection of Christ also discloses the condition and quality of the resurrectional life. In the age to come, we will not be restored simply to the present state. We will be brought into a new mode of existence, into something better and more perfect

(1 Cor 15.42-56). We will inherit not only Paradise from where we fell, but the heavens of heaven. The life we once experienced and lived will be raised up, in order to be clothed in immortality, "become perfect and irreversible . . . and attain the state in which it ought to have had, had not sin and the Fall entered the world."[221]

Through His exemplary life on earth Christ revealed the value of our earthly life for the achievement of salvation.[222] Through His resurrection He disclosed the ultimate worth and value of creation and affirmed its fundamental goodness. We are not saved from the material world but with it (Rom 8.18-23). The whole body of creation rises by anticipation in Christ's body. Christ's body was not merely resuscitated. At the resurrection it was radically transformed and freed from all limitation. It was exalted and glorified. Thus, the resurrection constitutes the token of the glorious transfiguration of the world, and not its negation. The age to come will reveal the comprehensive renovation and glorification of the whole of creation, and not its annihilation.[223] The universe was created by Christ. It belongs to Him. It is His gift of life to us. Therefore, it belongs to us as well as coheirs of Christ.

God in His infinite wisdom and love for the world continues to pursue His redemptive purpose. Through His Church, He calls the world to share in the reconstruction and renewal begun with the incarnation of His Son, who is the beginning and end of all things. He is the "One who not only moves history from within its own unfolding, but who also moves existence even from within the multiplicity of created things, towards the true being which is true life and true communion . . . The truth of history lies in the future, and this is to be understood in an ontological sense: history is true, despite changes and decay, not just because it is a movement towards an end, but mainly because it is a movement from the end, since it is the end that gives it meaning."[224] Christ, who is the Resurrection, the Life and the Light of the world, draws the world towards Himself. He is its Telos. It is He who fills all things with meaning. Meliton of Sardis, in a Paschal homily written in the second century, rhetorically put the following words in the mouth of Christ, to explain the wondrous mystery of our salvation:

> Come to me all you families of humankind sullied with sin, and
> receive the remission of your sins. For I am your forgiveness,
> I am the Pascha of salvation. I am the lamb immolated for you.
> I am your redemption. I am your life. I am your resurrection.
> I am your light. I am your salvation. I am your king. I lead you
> to the heights of heaven. I will show you the Father eternal. I
> will raise you by my right hand.

In the early Church, Pascha was considered the most appropriate time for conferring the sacraments of baptism, chrismation and the Eucharist, by which salvation is made one's own personal gift. Through the celebration of the baptsimal rites, the
Church realizes the cosmic significance of Christ's resurrection.
Christ, our true Passover, has made possible our passage from
death to life and from the world of sin to the life of God. At every
Divine Liturgy we experience and celebrate the certainty of Christ's
resurrection and live out its implications. We renew repeatedly
our baptismal pledge and are formed continuously into the body
of Christ. Filled with incomparable hope, we are called to faith
and to a mission: to transform both ourselves and the world by
furthering the Kingdom of God within us and within the world.

The joyous Paschal greeting, "Christ is Risen — Χριστὸς
'Ανέστη,'' with which we greet and embrace each other during
the season of Pascha, is never casual or empty. It speaks loudly
of God's immeasurable love for the world; the life-giving sacrifice
of His Son; the marvelous restoration of creation; and the newness
of life to which we have been called. It speaks to us as well about
our need to abandon our blind and selfish ways and surrender
ourselves and each other to the risen Lord. Father Dumitru
Staniloae sums it up with these penetrating words: ''. . . just as
in beholding his incarnate Son the Father sees and loves us all
as sons and adopts us through the incarnation of his Son, then
it is plain that in the face of every man we must see and love some
aspect of the face of Christ, indeed the very face of Christ himself.
Or to state the matter more precisely, every face is potentially
a face of Christ; that it is able to become a real face of Christ is

due to the fact that Christ has placed his image there, and it has become transparent of him. But we too have a part to play in the passage of each human face from this potential state to one in which it is truly the face of Christ."[225]

> Christ, the joy of all, the truth, the light, the life, the resurrection of the world, in His love appeared to those on earth; and He became Himself the pattern of our resurrection, granting divine forgiveness unto all.
>
> *(Kontakion, Saturday of Lazaros)*

> It is the day of Resurrection; let us be glorious in splendor for the festival, and let us embrace one another. Let us speak also, O brethren, to those who hate us, and in the Resurrection let us forgive all things, and so let us cry: Christ has risen from the dead, by death trampling upon death, and has bestowed life upon those in the tombs.
>
> *(Doxastikon)*

GENERAL OBSERVATIONS

The Development of the Paschal Vigil: History and Practice

The Paschal Vigil can be traced to the practice of the early Church to hold vigil on the night of the observance of Christ's resurrection. The structure, content and order of the Vigil developed gradually and over a considerable period of time. In its fullest form the Vigil was comprised of several services, that began on the evening of Great Saturday and lasted until the early morning of Pascha-Sunday. At Constantinople, e.g., the Paschal Vigil included the following series of services: The Great Paschal Vespers with the Divine Liturgy of St. Basil; the baptism of catechumens;[226] a ponderous recitation of the Acts of the Apostles; the Pannychis; the Intermediate Service (which is a more recent development); the Paschal Orthros; and the Divine Liturgy of St. John Chrysostom.

By the fifteenth century, as we have noted above, the revised Typikon of St. Savas had become the accepted regulator of liturgical practice throughout the Orthodox Church. This Typikon was first printed in 1545. In fact, the appearance of printed liturgical texts throughout the sixteenth century solidified the predominance of the monastic liturgical tradition and brought about as well a standarization of the divine services. This standardization, however, never became absolute. Omissions, abbreviations, variations and additions were inevitable, especially in parish usage. This condition of relative diversity resulted in the formulation of the new Typika of 1838 and 1888, the latter playing the decisive role in creating a new standard for liturgical practices. Thus, the printed Typika of 1545 and 1888 are essential departure points for our knowledge of the history and continued development of the Orthodox liturgical tradition in general and the services of Great Week and Pascha in particular.

Though it is not immediately evident, because of the disconnectedness of its several parts, the Paschal vigil we know and celebrate today is based essentially on the 1545 printed version of the Typikon of St. Savas, as modified later by the 1888 Typikon of the Great Church of Christ. The prevailing printed editions of the Triodion-Pentekostarion represent the monastic liturgical tradition that eventually shaped the 1545 printed Typikon. The volume, on the other hand, of the Holy and Great Week authorized and published by the Ecumenical Patriarchate in 1906, represents the modified version of that tradition, as embodied in the Typikon of 1888.

The direct and indirect antecedents of these Typika are to be found especially in the manuscripts of the Sabbite and Studite traditions and the Cathedral offices of Constantinople and Jerusalem. With regards to the development of the Paschal Vigil the essential comprehensive examination of these sources has been accomplished by Fr. Gabriel Bertoniere in his definitive study, *The Historical Development of the Easter Vigil and Related Service in the Greek Church.*[227]

The following table gives a general outline of the order of the Services of the Paschal Vigil according to the Typikon of 1545 and 1888.

The Printed Typika of 1545 and 1888

The Typikon of 1545[228]

Vespers:

— Around the tenth hour,[229] Vespers are begun in the usual way.

— The hymns accompanying the Evening Psalms include the resurrectional stichera of the first tone as well as the three paschal stichera (Σήμερον . . .).

— The Entrance, as usual.

— The Readings:

— There is no prokeimenon.

— The fifteen pericopes of the Constantinopolitan lectionary.

— The only song element is the Ode of the Three Children, which is sung not with the earlier scriptural refrain but with an adapted one: "Τὸν Κύριον ὑμνεῖτε . . ."

The Typikon of 1888[230]

Vespers:

— The Vespers are begun on Great Saturday morning (either after the Orthros; or separate from it, if the Orthros was sung on Great Friday night).

— The order of the Service is the same as the one in the printed Typikon of 1545.

— The Patriarch presides and reads the Προοιμιακός.

— The Readings:

— There is no prokeimenon.

— Only 3 of the 15 pericopes are read: Gen 1.1-5; Jonah 1-4; and Dan 3.1-56.

— The Ode of the Three Children (Dan 3.57-88) follows, with the refrain, "Τὸν Κύριον ὑμνεῖτε . . ." sung in the first tone.

The Typikon of 1545

The Divine Liturgy of St. Basil:

— Small Synapte.
— The Trisagion Prayer and Baptismal Trisagion.
— The Prokeimenon (Ps 65); Epistle and Gospel of the Constantinopolitan lectionary; before the Gospel, instead of the Alleluia, Ps 81 is sung with five stichoi.
— Instead of the Cherubikon, "Σιγησάτω πᾶσα σὰρξ βροτεία" (this is optional).
— The Communion hymn is "'Εξηγέρθη."
— The Apolysis takes place around the second hour of the night.
— The Antidoron is distributed.

The Typikon of 1888

The Divine Liturgy of St. Basil:

— The elements are the same as in the printed Typikon of 1545.
— The 1888 Typikon indicates that the "'Ανάστα ὁ Θεός" (Ps 81) is to be sung in the Grave (Βαρύς) tone.
— While this is being sung the priest strews laurel leaves throughout the Church, beginning with the Sanctuary.
— The Readings are the same.
— Instead of the Cherubikon, we sing the "Σιγησάτω" (in the Plagal of the First tone). The whole text is given.[231]
— The Κοινωνικόν: "'Εξηγέρθη."
— Instead of "Εἴδομεν τὸ φῶς, we sing the hymn, "Μνήσθητι εὔσπλαγχνε" (in the Second tone). The whole text is given.
— The Εἴη τὸ ὄνομα Κυρίου.
— The Apolysis is with the prologue "'Ο 'Αναστὰς ἐκ νεκρῶν," "because the Vespers of the Great Sunday (Pascha) have preceded the Liturgy."(!)
[Immediately after these entries, the Typikon lists the rubrics for the divine services in the Pentecostarion, beginning with the Great Sunday of Pascha. Thus, the Vesperal Liturgy has been assigned to the

The Typikon of 1545
The Meal:

— After the Divine Liturgy, the monks sit in their stalls and receive a light meal consisting of figs, dates, bread and wine.
— During the meal the Book of Acts is read.
— Afterwards the candles are lit and the semandra[232] are rung.

The Pannychis:

— The fixed elements of the Enarxis.
— The Canon of Great Saturday.
— After the 3rd Ode, the Kathisma and a specified reading from the Fathers.
— After the 6th Ode, the Kontakion and the second specified reading.
— After the 9th Ode there follow the Trisagion, Apolytikion ("Ὅτε κατῆλθες"), the Fervent Litany, and the Apolysis.

The Typikon of 1888

Triodion. Removed from its original moorings in the Vigil, it is now thought to be part of the paramone (παραμονή) of the feast of Pascha.]

The Pannychis:

— (It should be noted that the Typikon of 1888 does not name this service. I have inserted the title for purposes of clarity. Also, many printed editions of the service refer to it as the Pannychis).
— The service begins around the fifth hour of the night.
— The Enarxis:
— "Blessed is our God," "Heavenly King," and Trisagion Prayers.
— Kyrie, eleison (12) and Ps 50, preceded by the call to worship.
— The Canon of Great Saturday, "Κύματι θαλάσσης." Each hymn is introduced by the verse "Δόξα σοι ὁ Θεὸς ἡμῶν δόξα σοι." The Kathisma is not said.
— At the 4th Ode the Patriarch descends from the throne and prepares for the Divine Liturgy in the usual manner.
— The clergy vest.
— After the 9th Ode, from within the sanctuary the following are said: ""Ὅτε κατῆλθες""; the Fervent Litany; and the Apolysis.

The Typikon of 1545
[Intermediate Ceremonies]:

— At the conclusion of the Pannychis, all go to the Narthex.

— The lamplighter (κανδηλανάπτης) remains in the Church to light all the lamps and candles, and prepares the two fixed incense burners (one in the middle of the Church, the other by the Holy Doors).

— The priest vests in white, procedes to the Narthex, and censes the assembly.

— The Hegoumenos distributes candles; they are lit.

The Typikon of 1888
The Intermediate Service:

[a. *The Light*:
— At this point, between the Apolysis of the Pannychis and the Procession, the Typikon adds the following important detail in a footnote: "It is customary, at this point, in some places for the celebrating hierarch to stand at the Holy Doors holding the dikerotrikeron lit from the sleepless lamp (ἀκοίμητος κανδήλα) which rests upon the Holy Table. Singing the (hymn) 'Δεῦτε λάβετε φῶς ἐκ τοῦ ἀνεσπέρου φωτός', he invites the people to light their candles.[233]

b. *The Procession*:
— At the conclusion of the Pannychis service, the Patriarch, preceded by the hierarchs and clergy, leaves the sanctuary and procedes to the designated but unnamed place outside the Church, where there is a platform. During the procession the hymn, "Τὴν ἀνάστασίν σου," is sung.

— The Archdeacon bids the people to hear the Holy Gospel.

— The Patriarch then reads the designated pericope, Mt 28.1-20. [A footnote, at this point, indicates the following variants: First, some hierarchs and priests leave out verses 11-16 of the pericope; and second, in some Churches, both in

The Typikon of 1545
The Orthros:

— The Orthros begins when the aforementioned ceremonies have been concluded.

— The Enarxis.

— The "Χριστὸς 'Ανέστη" is sung ten times.

— The Royal Doors leading to the nave are opened and all enter. The priest proceeds into the sanctuary, from where he intones the Great Synapte.

— The Canon is then sung. After each Ode the Small Litany is intoned.

— The Hypakoe is sung after the 3rd Ode; while the Kontakion and Oikos are sung after the 6th Ode.

— A Reading from St. Gregory the Theologian follows at the conclusion of which the "'Ανάστασιν Χριστοῦ θεασάμενοι" is said.

— The Exaposteilarion is sung thrice after the 9th Ode and the Small Litany.

— The Ainoi follow with the four resurrectional stichera of the First tone.

— The four paschal stichera follow preceded by the prescribed verses from Ps 67 (2; 3ab; 3c-4a) and Ps 117 (24).

— The last of the four paschal stichera is repeated at the "Δόξα."

— The "Καὶ νῦν" is "'Αναστάσεως ἡμέρα."

The Typikon of 1888

in cities and monasteries, the practice is to read a different pericope, the Second Morning Gospel (i.e. Mk 16.1-8).][234]

The Orthros:[235]

— When the pericope is read the Patriarch censes the Gospel thrice, and having said the opening doxology, "Δόξα τῇ ἁγίᾳ καὶ ὁμοουσίῳ καὶ ζωοποιῷ καὶ ἀδιαιρέτῳ Τριάδι," he sings the hymn "Χριστὸς 'Ανέστη" thrice. The choirs repeat it six more times, while the Patriarch intones before each the prescribed verses from Pss 67 and 117. The Patriarch then sings it one more time, as he censes the clergy and the people.

— The Archdeacon says the Great Synapte; and the Patriarch says the ekphonesis.

— The procession into the Church begins, as the Patriarch sings the first hymn of the first Ode of the Canon of Pascha, "'Αναστάσεως ἡμέρα." Before each hymn of the series (except the εἱρμός) a verse is intoned, "Δόξα τῇ ἁγίᾳ ἀναστάσει σου Κύριε." The "Δόξα" and the "Καὶ νῦν" are said before the last two hymns of each series.

— The Typikon then lists the ekphonesis of the Small Litany after each Ode of the Canon. After the 3rd Ode the Hypakoe is

The Typikon of 1545

The Typikon of 1888

read (not sung).

— After the 6th Ode the Kontakion, the Oikos, and the Hypomnema of the day are read.

— Then the "'Ανάστασιν Χριστοῦ θεασάμενοι" is said thrice (once by the Patriarch and twice by two of the co-celebrating Hierarchs).

— Then the 7th, 8th, and 9th Odes are sung. The hymns of the 9th Ode are preceded by a Megalynarion. The Typikon lists six such verses. A seventh verse is sung before the Katavasia.

— The Small Litany; the Exaposteilarion (thrice); and the Ainoi follow. The hymns of the Ainoi are eight, the four resurrectional stichera of the First tone, and the four Paschal stichera, each preceded by the prescribed verses.

— The "Δόξα καὶ νῦν" is "'Αναστάσεως ἡμέρα."

The Kiss of Peace:

and the Apolysis follow:

— The kiss of peace is exchanged at the Holy Doors between the priest, deacon, proestos, and the brethren. After kissing the Gospel, each one kisses first the priest, then the proestos, then the rest of the brethren. The "Χριστὸς 'Ανέστη" is sung during the ceremony.

— The proestos then reads the "Κατηχητικὸς Λόγος" attributed to Saint John Chrysostom.

— The Fervent Litany and the Apolysis follow.

[A Modified Version of the Kiss of Peace]:

[The Typikon, by way of a footnote, indicates that the Gospel is presented for veneration at this point in the service — γίνεται ὁ ἀσπασμὸς τοῦ Εὐαγγελίου. It is also noted that in some places, the Gospel is presented at an earlier point in the service, at the beginning of the Canon for the convenience of both the clergy and the

The Typikon of 1545	The Typikon of 1888
	people. Probably, this was done in order to maintain the proper decorum. No mention, however, is made of an exchange of the kiss of peace.[236]

The Morning Liturgy of St. John Chrysostom:	**The Morning Liturgy of St. John Chrysostom:**

— The Enarxis (with "Χριστὸς 'Ανέστη").
— The Three Antiphons (Pss 65, 66, 67).
— The Εἰσοδικόν. Then the "Χριστὸς 'Ανέστη," the Hypakoe, and Kontakion after the Entrance.
— The Baptismal Trisagion.
— The Prokeimenon (Ps 117).
— The Readings (Acts 1.1-8; The Alleluia, Ps 101; Jn 1.1-17).
— The Cherubikon.
— The Κοινωνικόν : "Σῶμα Χριστοῦ."
— The "Χριστὸς 'Ανέστη" replaces the "Εἴη τὸ ὄνομα Κυρίου." (It also replaces Pss. 33 and 144, which followed the Divine Liturgy in the Monasteries.).

— Begins immediately at the conclusion of the Orthros.
— The Enarxis. The "Χριστὸς 'Ανέστη" is sung ten times, as at the beginning of the Orthros.
— The three Antiphons (Pss 65, 66, 67).
— The Εἰσοδικόν — "'Εν 'Εχκλησίαις εὐλογεῖτε τὸν Θεόν, Κύριον ἐκ πηγῶν 'Ισραήλ . . ." (A footnote indicates that this is sung everyday until the Apodosis of Pascha.).[237] Then the "Χριστὸς Ανέστη," the Hypakoe, and the Kontakion after the Entrace.
— The Baptismal Trisagion. (A footnote indicates that it is sung throughout the New Week and on the Apodosis).[238]
— The Apostolos. The Alleluia. The Gospel (Acts 1.1-8; Jn 1.1-17).
— At the "'Εξαιρέτως," the Katavasia of the 9th Ode is sung preceded by its verse.
— The Koinonikon — "Σῶμα Χριστοῦ."
— After the Prayer behind the Amvon, the "Χριστὸς 'Ανέστη" is said

The Typikon of 1545

The Typikon of 1888

thrice. (A footnote indicates that this is said throughout New Week. From the Sunday of Thomas the "Εἴη τὸ ὄνομα Κυρίου" is said).[239]

— Then the Patriarch reads the "Κατηχητικὸς Λόγος" of St. John Chrysostom (A footnote says that in the ancient Typika this homily was read after the Ainoi and before the Divine Liturgy, because it refers to the preparation of the faithful for the Divine Liturgy and Holy Communion. It is noted, however, that it had already become the practice to read it after the Koinonikon. The apolytikion of St. John Chrysostom is sung at the conclusion of the homily.)[240]

— Then comes the "Εὐλογία Κυρίου and the Apolysis. At the end of the Apolysis the Patriarch says "Χριστὸς Ἀνέστη" thrice, to which the people respond "Ἀληθῶς Ἀνέστη." The Patriarch then says "Δόξα τῇ Αὐτοῦ τριημέρῳ ἐγέρσει" and the people respond "Προσκυνοῦμεν Αὐτοῦ τὴν τριήμερον ἔγερσιν." Then the Patriarch (sings) the "Χριστὸς Ἀνέστη."

— The Patriarch and hierarchs then process to the Synodikon, preceded by candles, the hexapteryga, and the chanters. There, according to tradition, the Polychronismos of the Patriarch is sung.

The Dismantlement of the Early and Medieval Paschal Vigil

A lengthy Paschal Vigil appears to have been normative for many centuries. However, with the passage of time and for a variety of reasons the vigil began to break apart, especially in parish usage. Contributing to its fragmentation, were such things as the emergence of infant baptism, changing liturgical habits, modified fasting practices, a decreasing number of clerics, et al. As the vigil began to disintegrate some of its components were dislodged and displaced, while others withered and disappeared. In the process, a reduced and modified form of the vigil began to emerge. Though condensed and compressed, the vigil still retains its essential solemn, majestic, imposing, and joyful character. It remains as the most important, impressive and joyous celebration of the liturgical year.

The first step in the modification of the Paschal Vigil occurred when the Vesperal Divine Liturgy was distanced from the vigil. The Liturgy was moved initially to the late afternoon hours. Then it was lodged in the morning hours of Great Saturday.

Whatever the reasons for dislocating the Vesperal Liturgy, one thing is certain. The change represents a radical departure from the practice of the early Church, as well as a serious, though unintentional, distortion of the meaning of Great Saturday. By moving the Vesperal Liturgy to the morning hours of Great Saturday, we have inadvertently confused the liturgical commemorations related to the decisive and crucial three days of sacred history. Great Saturday is a day of gloom and watchful expectation. It is a day of profound silence; it has no eucharistic celebration. However, this fact becomes both blurred and mute, since a Liturgy is now celebrated on the morning of Great Saturday. Furthermore, this Liturgy is definitely Paschal in character and content. The prevailing liturgical practice, therefore, constitutes a contradiction and is untenable. To what extent the Church should or can restore this Vesperal Liturgy to its proper place remains an open question. The task, were it to be undertaken, is complex and difficult; but not impossible.

The New Intermediate Service

As the older elements of the Paschal Vigil were being altered and condensed, two new rites began to emerge. These rites would impact greatly on the present form of the Vigil.

The first rite is related to the lighting of the Paschal candle; the second to the introduction of a Gospel pericope pertaining to the resurrection. The lighting of the Paschal candles comes after the Pannychis, while the Gospel pericope is read before the Orthros. The two rites are linked to each other by a procession of the clergy and the people to a designated place outside the Church. Curiously enough, these two rites are not connected to either of the two services that frame them, the Pannychis and the Orthros. Together the two rites constitute a new "Intermediate Service" which has become the focus of much attention in popular piety and devotion. From information provided in the comparative tables above, we can say that the form of this brief new intermediate service, as we know and practice it today, came into existence only at the turn of this century. The antecedents of its two elements, however, are older.

The Light

The custom of lighting candles is rooted in the early Christian practice of lighting lamps each evening and morning in praise of Christ, who is the "Joyful light — Φῶς Ἱλαρόν."

More specifically, the present custom of lighting candles at Pascha has its beginnings in the practice of the Jerusalem Church.[241] Two traditions converged to shape this practice. First, it was customary throughout the early Church to light lamps at the Vesper service. Second, it had become the practice to strike a new flame at Pascha.

During the course of the tenth-eleventh centuries these two ceremonies took on greater ritual solemnity at Pascha in the Cathedral Church of Jerusalem. This Church is known as the Anastasis, or the Holy Sepulcher. It had come to be believed that the new light was produced miraculously. This light was referred to as the "Ἅγιον Φῶς — Holy Light."[242]

According to the early Typika, after the Old Testament readings of the paschal vespers, the Patriarch of Jerusalem would enter the Holy Tomb, offer prayers, take light from within the Tomb, and offer it to the Archdeacon, who in turn offered it to the people.

Surprisingly, as Bertoniere has pointed out, this Jerusalem ceremony has left no trace in other documents.[243] However, the rite to some extent was imitated in the monasteries and in churches.

The printed Typikon of 1545 indicates that at the conclusion of the Paschal Pannychis and before the Orthros, the monks assembled in the Narthex, where having received candles from the Hegoumenos, they lit them.[244] The lighting of the candles was meant to symbolize the resurrection of Christ.[245]

This simple ritual act, which had become commonplace, later became the basis for the present ceremony of the light. In an attempt to parallel the Jerusalem practice, it was embellished with ritual action and song.[246]

The present ceremony takes place at the conclusion of the Pannychis. The faithful hold candles, but do not leave the Church. At the appointed time, the celebrant takes the light from the "the sleepless lamp — ἀκοίμητος κανδήλα," that usually rests upon the Holy Table. (According to a long liturgical tradition the Holy Table is, among other things, symbolic of the Lord's Tomb.)[247] Then, while chanting the "Δεῦτε λάβετε φῶς — Come ye and receive light" hymn, the celebrant offers the light to the people. Here, the parallel with the Jerusalem practice is clear.

This hymn, — "Δεῦτε λάβετε φῶς ἐκ τοῦ ἀνεσπέρου φωτὸς καὶ δοξάσατε Χριστὸν τὸν Ἀναστάντα ἐκ νεκρῶν — Come ye and receive light from the unwaning light, and glorify Christ, who arose from the dead" — with its theme of light, is also reminiscent of the Jerusalem practice.

Significantly, the ceremony of the light was not incorporated into the text of the new Typikon of 1888. Nevertheless, the ceremony was being practiced in many places. The new Typikon makes mention of this fact, albeit in a footnote.[248] By the end of the century it had become a common practice, as evidenced by its inclusion in the Patriarchal Text of the Holy and Great Week.[249]

The ceremony of the light gained quick approval and popularity. Simple yet dramatic, it has captured the hearts of the people for its rich, moving and powerful symbolism: the risen and reigning Christ brings to the world the gift of light and everlasting life.

Christ, victorious over death and all the hostile powers that plague
humanity and hold it in bondage, dispels the darkness. He is the
light that shines in the darkness; the light of the world and the
life and light of men. (Jn 1; 4-5).

The Gospel

The Intermediate Service contains one more important element, the reading of a pericope from the Gospel giving an account of the resurrection. In the early documents, which contain
the new Intermediate Service, the designated pericope is Mt
28.1-20, the same as the Paschal Vigil Vespers. Later documents,
however, contain another pericope, or at least indicate it as a
variant reading. In time, this second pericope, Mk 16.1-8,[250]
prevailed and became the established reading, at least in most
places.[251]

The Gospel pericope in the intermediate service is especially
interesting because of its peculiar and unique position. It is not
part of the service that preceded it, nor is it part of the service
that follows it. Unlike all other Scripture lessons, it stands alone,
apart from and outside the context of a prescribed service. This
indicates that the Gospel pericope at this point in the service is
clearly an interpolation. When and why was this new element in-
terposed in the Vigil?

The first mention of this practice is made in a Typikon of the
Monastery of Philotheou at Mt. Athos, dated 1813.[252] Two
Typika, also from Mt. Athos, dated respectively 1850 from the
Monastery of St. Paul and 1869 from the Monastery of Vatope-
dion also mention the practice.[253] The custom spread and gained
in popularity. It passed into the 1888 printed Typikon of the Great
Church. This action formalized the practice and ensured its
dissemination and permanence.

None of the ancient Typika contain such a reading. In fact,
none of these Typika specify any pericopes for the Paschal Pannychis or Orthros. Only two medieval Typika, one from the tenth-
eleventh centuries and another dated 1292 have a Gospel reading
for the Orthros.[254] The first, places the reading at the end of the
service, while the other has it at the beginning of the service before

the Canon. However, these two documents are the exception and not the rule.

The absence of a Gospel lesson pertaining to the event of the resurrection of Christ in either the Pannychis or the Orthros probably brought about the introduction of the pericope in the intermediate service. The transfer of the Vesperal Divine Liturgy to the morning hours of Great Saturday had left the Paschal Vigil without a Gospel pericope on the resurrection. The Gospel lesson of the morning Divine Liturgy of St. John Chrysostom that follows the Paschal Orthros begins the course of the readings of the Gospel of John. The pericope of the morning Liturgy is taken from the prologue of the Gospel of John (1.1-17) and not from the narratives of the resurrection. Thus, to fill the void a new element was introduced into the Paschal Vigil. Strangely, the reading was not lodged in the Orthros, but placed before it. In this unique liturgical position, the Gospel pericope now serves as an announcement of the resurrection, which according to the Scriptures occured very early on the first day of the week.[255] Since the Paschal Orthros traditionally began well after midnight, the "new" Gospel reading not only announced, but in some respects, coincided with the event of the resurrection. Thus, the Orthros and Liturgy that follow are now viewed as the joyous celebration of the Event.

Further Alterations

The most critical change in the structure and meaning of the Paschal Vigil occured when the Vesperal Divine Liturgy was transposed to the morning hours of Great Saturday. Inevitably, this change brought with it a blurring of the meaning of Great Saturday and a confusion as to the nature, character and purpose of the Divine Liturgy in question.

Also, the emergence of infant baptism together with the slow disappearance of an effective catechumenate caused other changes in the earlier form of the Paschal Vigil. The most significant of these was the gradual disappearance of the baptismal rites from the sequence of the services at the Vigil. This had a double effect. On the one hand, the Paschal celebration was robbed of an important theological dimension and perspective, and on the other, it lost one of its major liturgical components.

As a consequence, other elements of the Vigil also started to wane. The course of the fifteen Old Testament Readings in the Vesper service is a case in point. The tenth century Typikon of the Great Church informs us that several of these pericopes were omitted if the baptismal rites were completed before the Readings were finished.

While the full course of the fifteen Readings was retained in the monastic practice, the 1888 Typikon limited the pericopes to three, Gen 1.1-13; Jonah 1-4; and Daniel 3.1-56. It is also signifi- cant that both the 1545 and the 1888 printed Typika dropped all the song elements from these readings, except for the final Ode of the Three Children.

The long ponderous reading of the Book of Acts, characteristic of the monastic practice, never really took root in parish usage and fell into disuse in most places.

The form of the Pannychis in parish usage has been gradual- ly simplified and shortened. For example, except for the eirmos, the hymns in each Ode are no longer said more than once. The 1888 Typikon also omitted the Kathismata, as well as the readings from Patristic texts.

RUBRICS

The Vesperal Liturgy of St. Basil[256]

Preliminaries

The Vesperal Liturgy once marked the beginning of the Paschal Vigil. In current usage, however, this Liturgy is celebrated on Great Saturday morning. The service is comprised of two main parts: the Great Vespers of Pascha and the Divine Liturgy. The hymns and the Readings are replete with baptismal and resurrectional motifs, which are reflective of the character of the service, as well as its original position and setting in the Paschal Vigil.

Because this is a Paschal Liturgy the priest wears bright vestments (white or gold). The Holy Table also is covered with a bright cloth.

The Kairos is conducted before the Service; and the Pros- komide may be conducted before or during the Vespers.

The Vespers

The first part of the Vespers is conducted in the usual manner and in accordance with the rubrics of a Great Vesper Service. The order is recorded in the Patriarchal Text.

The priest, vested fully, begins the service with the opening doxology, "Blessed is the Kingdom." The service continues in the usual order. The priest censes as usual during the singing of the Evening Psalms.

At the Entrance, the priest holds the Gospel. (He may wish to carry the censer as well.) The "Φῶς ἱλαρόν — Joyful Light" is sung.

The Readings commence immediately after the "Φῶς ἱλαρόν." There is no prokeimenon. In current usage we read only three of the fifteen Old Testament pericopes listed in the Triodion. The Patriarchal Text designates the following pericopes: the first (Genesis); the fourth (Jonah) and the fifteenth (Daniel).

When the Readings have been completed the choir sings the Hymn of the Three Children. The people respond after each verse, singing the refrain "Τὸν Κύριον ὑμνεῖτε καὶ ὑπερυφοῦτε εἰς πάντας τοὺς αἰῶνας — Praise the Lord and exalt Him unto the ages."

The Divine Liturgy

When the Hymn of the Three Children is completed the priest says, "Τοῦ Κυρίου δεηθῶμεν — Let us pray to the Lord." This signals the beginning of the Divine Liturgy of St. Basil. The priest reads the Prayer of the Trisagion.

Instead of the regular Trisagion the choir sings the Baptismal Trisagion, ""Οσοι εἰς Χριστόν — As many as have been baptized into Christ. . . ."

The reading of the Apostolos follows. When the Epistle lesson has been concluded, the Alleluia is not sung. Instead, the priest sings the refrain, "'Ανάστα ὁ Θεὸς κρῖνον τὴν γῆν — Arise, O God, and judge the earth . . . " (Ps 81.8). The choir sings Ps 81, repeating the refrain after each verse.

Around the fourteenth-fifteenth centuries a new ritual was introduced into the Paschal Vigil, in order to emphasize the triumph of God over His enemies through the resurrection of Christ. While

Ps 81 is being sung the priest conducts *the ritual of spreading laurel leaves*[257] throughout the Church. The ceremony is seen a sign of victory and as an expression of joy.

During the singing of Ps 81 the priest takes a basket filled with laurel leaves (or other appropriate leaves) and scatters them by hand in the sanctuary and throughout the Church. While the leaves are being strewn, it has become customary in many places to ring bells, thus adding to the joyous character of the ritual.[258]

When the Psalm is concluded the priest reads the Gospel in the usual way.

The Epistle and Gospel pericopes together with their respective prokeimena Ps 65 and Ps 81, bring into sharp focus the resurrection of Christ and its cosmic significance.

Instead of the regular Cherubikon the choir sings "Σιγησάτω πᾶσα σὰρξ βροτεία — Let all mortal flesh keep silence." The Communion Hymn is "Ἐξηγέρθη ὡς ὁ ὑπνῶν — The Lord has waked as if from sleep."

Instead of "Εἴδομεν τὸ φῶς — We have seen the light," we sing "Μνήσθητι εὔσπλαγχνε . . . — Remember us. . . ." The prologue of the Apolysis is "Ὁ Ἀναστὰς ἐκ νεκρῶν — May He who rose from the dead. . . ."

The Pannychis[259]

With the transfer of the Vesperal Liturgy to the morning hours, the Paschal Vigil now begins with the service of the Pannychis. In some books the Pannychis is titled the Paschal Mesonyktikon (or Midnight Service).

According to the prevailing practice the people gather in the Church around 11 o'clock on the night of Great Saturday.

The Holy Gate is opened. Vested with rason and epitrachelion, the priest begins the service of the Pannychis with the opening doxology, "Blessed is our God . . . — Εὐλογητὸς ὁ Θεὸς ἡμῶν . . ."; and the prayer "Heavenly King."

The Reader says the Trisagion Prayers; Lord have mercy (12); Glory . . . now and forever . . . and Psalm 50 (51).

Then the choir sings the whole Canon of Great Saturday, uninterrupted by priestly petitions. After the Third Ode of the

Canon the priest, having taken the Kairos, proceeds to put on his paschal vestments. The priest may, also, wish to begin the Proskomide during the Canon.

It has become customary in the Greek Orthodox Archdiocese for the priest to read the Paschal Encyclical before the Canon concludes. When the Canon has been completed, it has become customary for the chanters to retire into the sanctuary to join the priest for the concluding part of the Pannychis.

According to the prescribed order in the manuscripts, as well as the printed Typika and the Triodion, the Pannychis concludes as follows: After the Canon, the Trisagion ("῞Αγιος ο Θεός") is recited. Then the resurrectional apolytikion of the Second Tone ("῞Οτε κατῆλθες . . . When you descended . . .") is sung. The priest then intones the brief version of the Fervent Litany; followed by the Apolysis, with the resurrectional prologue.[260]

During the Service of the Pannychis the Church is kept dimly lit. In accordance with ancient customs,[261] the lamps and candles of the Church are extinguished before the Pannychis. The only lamp left burning is the "Sleepless Lamp" in the sanctuary; and whatever other candles, lamps or lights are absolutely essential. Except for the "Sleepless Lamp," these, too, are extinguished after the Canon and before the concluding part of the Pannychis.

The Intermediate Service

After the Apolysis of the Pannychis we commence what has come to be known as the Intermediate Service.

The Ceremony of the Light

The priest is in the sanctuary. He takes the Paschal Candle, and lighting it from the flame of the "Sleepless Lamp," he begins to sing, "Δεῦτε λάβετε φῶς . . . — Come ye and receive light . . . ." The Holy Gate opens and the priest brings the light to the people, while the choirs repeat the same hymn several times. When all have received the light, the lamps are lit and the lights are turned on.

The Procession

When all have received the light, the procession begins to the designated place where the Gospel will be read.

During the procession the choir sings the hymn, "Τὴν Ἀνάστασίν Σου Χριστὲ Σωτήρ . . ." — "Your resurrection Christ our Savior. . . ." The acolytes carrying candles, the hexepteryga, the Icon and the Banner (λάβαρον) of the Resurrection proceed first. They are followed by the Choir. The Priest follows, carrying the Gospel and the Paschal candle. The people follow.

The Gospel

It is customary to read the Resurrection narrative at an appointed place outside the Church. If this is not possible, the procession follows the usual route to the Narthex. The Gospel is read by the Central Door of the Narthex.

When the procession has come to the designated place, the priest bids the people to hear the holy Gospel, "Καὶ ὑπὲρ τοῦ κατα- ξιωθῆναι ἡμᾶς . . . Σοφία. Ὀρθοί," etc.

As we have noted above, it has become the custom to read the Second Morning Gospel (Mark 16.1-8), rather than the pericope designated by the Typikon (Matthew 28.1-20).

The Paschal Orthros

The Paschal Orthros commences immediately after the Gospel lesson of the Intermediate Service. The order is contained in the Patriarchal Text.

The Enarxis and the Great Synapte are said at the place where the Gospel was read. The priest censes the Gospel and says the opening doxology.

The Enarxis

    — The priest intones the opening doxology: "Δόξα τῇ ἁγία . . . — Glory to the holy, consubstantial . . . ."[262]

    — He then sings the "Χριστὸς Ἀνέστη . . . — Christ is risen . . ." three times. The last phrase is sung by the choir.

    — The priest intones the prescribed verses. The choir sings the refrain, "Χριστὸς Ἀνέστη." (four verses from Ps 67, the "δόξα," the "καὶ νῦν," and the refrain again by the priest. The refrain is sung ten times in all.).

— The priest says the Great Synapte.

The Canon of Pascha[263]

— Immediately after the litany, the choir sings the Canon of Pascha "'Ἀναστάσεως ἡμέρα . . . — It is the day of resurrection . . ." The hymns of each Ode are prefaced by the phrase "Δόξα τῇ ἁγίᾳ ἀναστάσει σου, Κύριε . . . Lord, glory to Your holy resurrection."

— The procession reforms and everyone returns to their appointed places, as the Canon is being sung.[264]

— At the indicated intervals the priest intones the Small Litany. The series of the doxological endings of the litany are found in the Patriarchal Text or the Ieratikon.

— After the third Ode the Hypakoe is read. After the sixth Ode we read: the Kontakion and Oikos of Pascha; the Synaxarion of the day and the Feast; the prayer "'Ἀνάστασιν Χριστοῦ θεασάμενοι . . . — Having beheld the resurrection of Christ . . ."; and the hymn, "'Ἀναστὰς ὁ 'Ιησοῦς . . . — Jesus having risen . . ."[265]

— Before the ninth Ode the priest intones "Τὴν Θεοτόκον καὶ Μητέρα . . . — Let us magnify the Theotokos and Mother . . ." and censes as usual during the singing of the Ode.

— The eirmos, the hymns and the katavasia of the ninth Ode are preceded by a series of megalynaria. The 1888 Typikon lists seven such verses. The 1985 edition of the Patriarchal Text published by the Apostolike Diakonia lists an additional five verses.[266]

The Exaposteilarion and Ainoi

— Following the Small Litany at the end of the Canon, the choir sings the Exaposteilarion, "Σαρκὶ ὑπνώσας . . . — King and Lord in the flesh Thou did sleep . . ." (thrice).

— The Psalms of Praise (Ainoi) and the two sets of the appointed hymns follow. First, we sing the four resurrectional hymns of the first tone, and then the four hymns of Pascha. The Paschal hymns are preceded by verses from Ps 67.

— The Doxastikon follows, "'Ἀναστάσεως ἡμέρα, καὶ λαμπρυνθῶμεν τῇ πανηγύρει . . . — It is the day of resurrection, let us be glorious in splendor for the festival. . . ." The hymn ends with the "Χριστὸς ᾽Ανέστη" (said three times).

While this Doxastikon is being chanted, in accordance with ancient custom, the faithful exchange the kiss of agape or peace.[267]

— The Paschal Orthros in its present form ends with the Doxastikon and the exchange of the kiss of peace.

The Morning Divine Liturgy

According to current practice we celebrate the Divine Liturgy of St. John Chrysostom immediately after the Orthros. Care should be taken to celebrate the service with splendor and joy.

The Enarxis to the Readings

— After the opening doxology, the rubrics indicate that the "Χριστὸς ᾽Ανέστη" is sung ten times in the manner noted above at the Orthros.

— The Psalms of the three Antiphons are 65, 66, and 67; and 117.24.

— The Εἰσοδικόν, or Entrance hymn, is "᾽Εν ἐκκλησίαις εὐλογεῖτε τὸν Θεόν. . . ."

— After the Entrance we sing the "Χριστὸς ᾽Ανέστη (1), the Hypakoe and the Kontakion.

— The Baptismal Trisagion is sung in the place of the regular Trisagion.

— The appointed readings are Acts 1.1-8 and John 1.1-17. The respective prokeimena are Pss 117 and 101.

— The homily of St. John Chrysostom may be read after the Gospel in the place of a sermon.[268]

From the Great Entrance to the Apolysis

— At the "᾽Εξαιρέτως" we sing the Katavasia of the ninth Ode prefaced by the megalynarion.

— The Communion hymn is "Σῶμα Χριστοῦ — The Body of Christ. . . ."

— Instead of the hymn "We have seen the true light" we sing the "Χριστὸς ᾽Ανέστη." The Paschal hymn is also sung in the place of "Blessed be the name of the Lord."[269]

— In the Apolysis we use the usual prologue for Sundays. The ending, however, is unique to Pascha. It concludes in a dialogue between the celebrant and the faithful. The form can be found in the Patriarchal Text and the Ἱερατικόν.

This form of the Apolysis is used throughout Renewal Week and on the feast of the Apodosis of Pascha. In some places it has become the custom to use this form throughout the Paschal season, in order to emphasize the joy and triumph of the resurrection. Instead of the "Δι' εὐχῶν" we say the "Χριστὸς Ἀνέστη."

The Holy Gate

The Holy Gate and the two side doors leading into the sanctuary remain open throughout Renewal Week (Διακαινίσιμος Ἑβδομάς). The Holy Gate is opened at the Ceremony of the Light; and stays open throughout the Paschal Season.

The Paschal Vespers

The solemn and joyous festivities of Great Week and Pascha end with the Great Vesper Service celebrated on the Sunday of Pascha. This service is often referred to as the Vespers of Agape.

Technically, the service should be celebrated in the afternoon. However, in most places it is conducted in the morning hours, in the place of a morning liturgy. The 1888 Typikon, reflecting the practices of the Church of Constantinople, orders the service to be conducted in the morning hours.[270]   The order of the service is found in the Pentecostarion and the Patriarchal Text.[271]

Vesting

— According to ancient custom the priest wears the full set of priestly vestments. The priest vests before the service.

— In some places it is customary for the clergy to vest in an adjacent building or room and to process to the Church for the service. Such is the case at the Patriarchal Church in Constantinople[272] and in monasteries. While the clergy vest the choir sings the "Ἀναστάσεως ἡμέρα." During the procession the choir sings the "Χριστὸς Ἀνέστη."

The Gospel Lesson

The Paschal Vespers contain only one reading; the Gospel pericope Jn 20.19-24, recounting the appearance of the risen Lord to His disciples on the evening of the day of the resurrection.

Traditionally, this pericope is read in several languages in order to emphasize the universality of the Gospel and the apostolicity and catholicity of the Church. The Good News is to be proclaimed boldly and joyously in every age and to all people. And the heart of the Gospel is to preach Jesus Christ crucified and risen.

Normally, only the clergy read the Gospel lessons in the divine services, according to our liturgical tradition and practice. An exception, however, is made at this service. In the absence of a sufficient number of clergy, qualified Orthodox lay persons are invited to read the appointed pericope in one of several languages.[273]

The pericope is divided into three sections. The celebrant invites the congregation to hear the holy Gospel in the usual manner. He procedes to read the first section. When he has concluded the first section, each reader in turn repeats the section. This same order is followed for the two subsequent sections.

The Order of the Service

The Enarxis

— The priest, fully vested, standing in front of the Holy Table and holding the thurible (censer), intones the opening doxology, "Δόξα τῇ ἁγίᾳ . . . — Glory to the holy, consubstantial. . . ."

— The "Χριστὸς Ἀνέστη" is chanted ten times, according to the order described above in the Orthros. While intoning the verses the priest moves around the Holy Table. He censes the Table on each side, the sanctuary, the icons, and the people, in the usual manner from the Holy Gate.[274]

— The Great Synapte follows.

The Evening Psalms and the Entrance

— After the Great Synapte the choir sings the Evening Psalms and the resurrectional hymns of the second tone. The priest censes in the usual manner at the "Κατευθυνθήτω."

— The entrance is conducted in the usual manner. The priest carries the Gospel.

— After the "Φῶς Ἱλαρόν" we sing the Great Prokeimenon, "Τίς Θεὸς μέγας . . ." (Ps 76).

The Gospel

— Following the Entrance and the Prokeimenon, the Priest and the appointed Readers read the Gospel pericope as noted above.

The Remainder of the Vesper Service

— Following the Gospel we say the Fervent Litany, the Evening "Prayer," the Dismissal litany, the Peace, and the Prayer for the bowing of heads.

— The choir sings the Aposticha (the first resurrectional apostichon hymn of the second tone and the four Paschal hymns). The "Δόξα" and "Καὶ νῦν," is "Ἀναστάσεως ἡμέρα."[275]

— The Apolysis follows in the manner described above at the morning Divine Liturgy.

Preaching The Word

The sermon is an essential part of worship. It is itself an act of prayer, a salvific and transforming event. Because the sermon helps to bring and build faith, preaching is one of the priest's most important responsibilities and tasks. The sermon engages the people with the fundamental truths of the Gospel. Preaching is a powerful force for sustaining faith, as well as for comforting, exhorting and inspiring the people. It is, therefore, of paramount importance that the priest be prepared to offer meaningful sermons at each divine service for the edification of the faithful.

* * * * *

NOTES

[1] The term Pascha (Πάσχα) is the Hellenized form of the Jewish word pesach, (or Phaska), which means passage or passover. It does not derive from the Greek verb πάσχω, to suffer, as some, like the ancient writer Meliton of Sardis, have thought. Meliton was inclined to associate the word Pascha with the verb pavscw, because, like his fellow Christians of Asia Minor, he was a Quartodeciman (literally a Four-teenthist). In the second century the churches of Asia Minor had come to relate the celebration of Pascha above all to the passion and death of Christ rather than to his resurrection. That is why they observed Pascha on the 14 day of Nisan, i.e., the day on which Christ was crucified (see below).

[2] See Bishop Demetrios Trakatellis, *Authority and Passion* (Brookline, 1987); and Raymond E. Brown, *The Birth of the Messiah* (New York, 1977). Note, e.g., the Apostle Peter's sermon at Pentecost (Acts 2.22-28) and his defense before the Council (Acts 5.29-32). Note also the commemoration in the Anaphora of the Divine Liturgies of St. Basil and St. John Chrysostom.

[3] The earliest evidence is found in *The Letter of the Apostles* (ca. 150 A.D.). Written originally in Greek, it survives only in Coptic and Ethiopian translations. See Edgar Hennecke, *New Testament Apocrypha* (London, 1963), pp. 190-91.

[4] See Thomas J. Talley, *The Origins of the Liturgical Year* (New York, 1986), p. 2. See also J. G. Davies, *Holy Week: A Short History* (Richmond, 1974). A. A. McArthur, *The Evolution of the Christian Year* (London, 1953). A. G. Mortimort, ed., *The Church at Prayer* 4 (Collegeville, 1986).

[5] The Jews used unleavened bread at the Passover. It was their custom to remove all yeast from their homes on the day before the Passover (the 14th day of Nisan). They ate unleavened bread (ἄζυμα — azymes) during the Passover festival (Exodus 12.1-20, and 13.3-10). See Anthony J. Saldarini, *Jesus and Passover* (New York, 1984), pp. 10, 34-36. See also D. Doikos, *Τὸ Βιβλικὸν Ἑβραϊκὸν Πάσχα* (Thessalonike, 1986). E. Antoniades, *Ὁ Χαρακτὴρ τοῦ Τελευταίου Δείπνου τοῦ Κυρίου καὶ ὁ Ἄρτος τῆς Θείας Εὐχαριστίας* (Athens, 1961).

[6] According to Jewish reckoning, each new day begins at sundown. It can be established that the primitive Church assembled on Saturday night for the celebration of the eucharist, following closely the Jewish pattern. Sacred meals were essentially supper meals related to the beginning of the day at evening. The eucharistic synaxis, like the Mystical (Last) Supper, was originally connected to a supper meal. This arrangement lasted at least until the end of the first or the early part of the second century, when for various reasons the original evening eucharistic synaxis was transferred first to the pre-dawn hours and later to the "third" hour of the day. For a discussion on the whole range of problems, issues and aspects pertaining to the time of the celebration of the Divine Liturgy in the worship of the Orthodox Church see A. Calivas, *Χρόνος Τελέσεως τῆς Θείας Λειτουργίας* (Analecta Vlatadon, 37, Thessalonike, 1982).

[7] 1 Cor 11.23-26. See also the Anaphora of the Divine Liturgy of St. Basil.

[8] See, e.g., *The Letter of the Apostles*, 15: "After my return to the Father you will celebrate the memory of my death . . . and (I) will come to you and join in the night vigil with you, and stay near you until cockcrow. When you then have ended your agape, the memorial of me which you make . . ." See *New Testament Apocrypha*, p. 199.

[9] See T. J. Talley, *The Origins of the Liturgical Year*, p. 6.

[10] See L. Sabourin, "Easter in the Early Church," *Religious Studies Bulletin* 2/1 (1982) 23-25. Veselin Kesich, *The Gospel Image of Christ* (Crestwood, 1972), pp. 56-60.

[11]We do not know the exact time of the resurrection. It happened at some point in the early morning hours of Sunday, the first day of the week. The Gospels only make reference to the time the first witnesses to the resurrection arrived at the empty tomb. Matthew tells us it was "toward the dawn" — Ὀψὲ δὲ σαββάτων, τῇ ἐπιφουσκούσῃ εἰς μίαν σαββάτων" (28.1); Mark says it was "very early" — "καὶ λίαν πρωῒ τῇ μιᾷ τῶν σαββάτων" (16.2); Luke says it was "early dawn" — "τῇ δὲ μιᾷ τῶν σαββάτων ὄρθρου βαθέως (24.1); John tells us it was "early, while it was still dark" — "πρωῒ σκοτία ἔτι οὔσης (20.1).

[12]According to Jewish custom, the Passover began on the evening of the 14th day of the first month, i.e., Nisan. The 14th of Nisan was the day of preparation for the Passover. The paschal lambs were slaughtered in the afternoon of that day in anticipation of the festival, which began at sundown. Since, in accordance to Jewish practice, each new day begins at sunset, the 15 of Nisan was the first day of the Passover. Jesus was resurrected after the first day of the Passover.

[13]For a fuller discussion on the date of Pascha see A. Calivas, "The Date of Pascha: The Need to Continue the Debate," *The Greek Orthodox Theological Review* 35/4 (1990) 333-43. According to the decree of the First Ecumentical Synod, the date of Pascha can only occur on a Sunday between March 22 and April 25. However, due to the descrepancy that exists in the Orthodox Church today because of the use of two calendars, the Julian (Old) and the Gregorian (New), the dates of March 22 and April 25 are superimposed on the new calendar. (March 22 in the New calendar reads April 3, while April 25 reads May 8. This reflects the 13 day difference between the two calendars.) In this way all Orthodox Christians celebrate Pascha on the same day, but not on the same date.

[14]Quoted by Eusebios, in his *Ecclesiastical History*, 5, 24, 12-17. According to ancient custom and practice, the faithful consumed only one frugal meal in the afternoon during fast days. The Great Week fast was observed by all with great solemnity. The length and the severity of the fast depended on local usage. In time, fasting practices would be influenced greatly by the monastic experience. For a discussion on the practice of fasting, see *The Lenten Triodion*, trans. Mother Mary and Kallistos Ware (London, 1978), pp. 28-37. C. Enisleides, Ὁ Θεσμὸς τῆς Νηστείας (Athens, 1969). J. F. Wimmer, *Fasting in the New Testament* (New York, 1982).

[15]See Dionysios of Alexandria, *Letter to Basileiades*, PG 10.1273-76.

[16]The Great Fast with its rich liturgical material developed over a long period of time. Two practices in the early Church were especially significant in its development. The one pertained to the preparation of catechumens for baptism and the other to the reconcilliation of lapsed Christians to the Church. Both practices were related to the Paschal feast.

[17]The forty day fast developed along different lines in the East and the West. For most of the East the two fast periods, though related, were separate and distinct. In the Western tradition, however, the forty days include the six day fast of Holy Week. The Great Fast seeks to make the Christian mindful of his/her dependence on God. It prepares each person for the worthy celebration of Pascha by calling all to repentance and to a deeper conversion of the heart. The Great Fast finds its completion in the solemn celebrations of the Great Week. For an excellent study on the formation and development of the Great Fast see Evangelos Theodorou, Η Μορφωτικὴ Ἀξία τοῦ Ἰσχύοντος Τριωδίου (Athens, 1958). See also A. Schmemann, *Great Lent* (Crestwood, 1974); and Archimandrite Kallistos, "Ἱστορικὴ Ἐπισκόπησις τοῦ Τριωδίου," *Νέα Σιών* 24 (1934).

[18]Adolf Adam, *The Liturgical Year* (New York, 1981), English translation by M. J.

O'Connell, p. 63.

[19]The daily cycle of worship contains the following services: Midnight (Mesonyktikon), Orthros, Hours (First, Third, Sixth, Ninth), Vespers, and Compline (Apodeipnon). For a brief explanation of these services see A. Calivas, *Come Before God* (Brookline, 1986). For a comprehensive study on the development of the daily office, see Robert Taft, *The Liturgy of the Hours in East and West* (Collegeville, 1986); Paul F. Bradshaw, *Daily Prayer in the Early Church* (New York, 1982). Also see Ioannis Fountoules, *Κείμενα Λειτουργικά* (Thessalonike, 1977).

[20]In addition to these four, the service books of the Church also include the: Archieratikon; Euchologion; Evangelion; Apostolos; Prophetologion; Psalter; Octoechos (or Parakletike); the collection of twelve volumes, one for each month, called the Menaia; and the Typikon. Of these, the Prophetologion practically has fallen into disuse. The Old Testament readings it contains for various occasions and services have been dispersed throughout the other liturgical books. In addition to the formal books mentioned above, there exists a small library of books which contain, e.g., a) separate volumes for each of the sacraments and other services taken from the Euchologion; and b) compilations of services taken from the various books. One such book is the Συνέκδημος or "companion," which is especially useful for the laity; and another is the "Holy and Great Week" about which we will speak below.

[21]The word 'triodion' means simply 'three odes' (τρεῖς ᾠδαί). The name is derived from the fact that many of the Canons in the Triodion have only three odes, instead of the usual nine. A Canon is a series of hymns, sung at the Orthros service. A Canon is based on the nine odes or canticles of the Bible (eight from the Old Testament, and two from the New, the latter being combined into one, the ninth ode). Canons have a varying number of hymns in each series. The first hymn in the series is called the eirmos, and is usually set apart by quotations. The eirmos (=series) sets the meter and melody of each hymn in the series. Also, the eirmos usually provides a brief poetical summary and a theological reflection of the particular Biblical Ode in the series. The final hymn of each series is called the Katavasia. Like the preceding hymns in the series the Katavasia provides theological reflections on a given theme. The Katavasia derives its name from action of the chanters who would "step down" from their stalls to sing the hymn in unison. Today, in parish practice, the Canon has been mostly suppressed (except for Great Week), and only the Katavasiai are chanted. It should be noted, too, that Canons occur in other services besides the Orthros.

[22]The Pentekostarion covers an eight-week period beginning with Pascha and ending with the Sunday of All Saints, which occurs one week after Pentecost, whence it gets its name.

[23]The word κατανυκτικός means "to prick the heart." In devotional language it means to cause repentance, by opening the heart of sinners to the mercy, love and joy of God, Who brings salvation and sanctifies life.

[24]The method by which the beginning of the day is reckoned appears to have had a significant impact on the formation of the observances of Great Week. Two such methods co-exist in the liturgical tradition of the Orthodox Church. One is of Judaic origin, while the other is Roman-Byzantine. According to the former, the day is reckoned from one sunset to the next. According to the latter, the day begins at midnight. It could be argued that the Roman-Byzantine method, which was incorporated into the laws of the Empire, became the dominant of the two methods. Accordingly, evening observances that once began the liturgical day (according to the Judaic practice), were seen more and more as celebrations of anticipation rather than part of the feast itself. As such, the evening observances of the great feasts acquired the characteristics of

a vigil. In the Constantinopolitan tradition these vesperal services were called παραμονή — paramone. The paramone consisted of solemn vespers with Scripture lessons. Sometimes, as in the case of Pascha, Christmas and Theophany, the paramone concluded with a Eucharist. Once the evening celebrations were no longer considered as the beginning of a particular festival, it became easier to dislodge them from their original setting. For a discussion on the subject of the method by which the beginning of the day is reckoned, see A. Calivas, "'Η 'Αρχὴ τῆς Νυχθημέρου καὶ ἡ Λατρεία τῆς 'Εκκλησίας, in *'Αναφορὰ εἰς Μνήμην Μητροπολίτου Σάρδεων Μαξίμου* 3 (Geneva, 1989) pp. 93-105. For a discussion on Cathedral Vigils and a description of the paramone, see R. Taft, *Liturgy of the Hours*, pp. 165-190 and especially p. 173.

[25]For further information on the development of the Triodion, see E. Theodorou, *'Η Μορφωτικὴ 'Αξία τοῦ 'Ισχύοντος Τριωδίου.*

[26]For additional information see P. N. Trembelas, *'Εκλογὴ 'Ελληνικῆς 'Ορθοδόξου 'Υμνογραφίας*" (Athens, 1949). N. P. Papadopoulos, "'Υμνογράφοι 'Αδεσπότων 'Εορτῶν in *'Εκκλησία* (1953) 109. K. Mitsakes, *Βυζαντινὴ 'Υμνογραφία* (Athens, 1986). A. Fitrakis, *'Η 'Εκκλησιαστικὴ ἡμῶν Ποίησις,* 1956. G. Florovsky, "Hymnographers, Polemicists and Florilegia" in his collected works, vol. 9, *The Byzantine Fathers of the Sixth to Eighth Century* (Belmont, 1987), pp. 19-34. H. J. W. Tillyard, *Byzantine Music and Hymnography* (London, 1923). E. Wellesz, *A History of Byzantine Music and Hymnography* (Oxford, 1961). S. J. Savas, *The Treasury of Orthodox Hymnology: Triodion* (Minneapolis, 1983). *The Lenten Triodion,* pp. 40-43. Dimitri Conomos, *Byzantine Hymnography and Byzantine Chant* (Brookline, 1984).

[27]The Typikon is the Book of directives and rubrics, which regulate the order of the divine services for each day of the year. It presupposes the existence of other liturgical books which contain the fixed and variable parts of these services. In the strict monastic sense, the Typikon of the monastery includes both the rule of life of the community as well as the rule of prayer.

[28]See A. Calivas, *Χρόνος Τελέσεως τῆς Θείας Λειτουργίας,* p. 197ff.

[29]On the development of the Typikon, as well as the origins of the daily services, see A. Schmemann, *Introduction to Liturgical Theology* (Crestwood, 1966 and 1986). M. Arranz, "Les grandes étapes de la Liturgie Byzantine; Palestine-Byzance-Russie. Essai d'aperçu historique," in *Liturgie de l'église particulière et liturgie de l'église universelle,* 43-72. BELS 7 (Rome: Edizion: Liturgiche, 1976). R. Taft, *The Liturgy of the Hours. The Study of Liturgy,* eds. Jones, Wainwright, and Yarnold, 1978, pp. 208-22 and 350-69. And A. Calivas, *Χρόνος Τελέσεως τῆς Θείας Λειτουργίας.* For the texts of various Typika see, Aleksej Dimitrievskij Opsionanie Liturgitseskich Rukopisej, Tupikav (Kiev, 1895 and Hildesheim, 1965); and A. Papadopoulos-Kerameus, *'Ανάλεκτα 'Ιεροσολυμιτῆς Σταχυολογίας* 2 (Petersburg, 1894). See also the: *Τυπικὸν 'Εκκλησιαστικὸν κατὰ τὸ ὕφος τῆς Χριστοῦ Μεγάλης 'Εκκλησίας, τοῦ Κωνσταντίνου Πρωτοψάλτου* (Constantinople, 1838). *Τυπικὸν τῆς τοῦ Χριστοῦ Μεγάλης 'Εκκλησίας, τοῦ Γεωργίου Βιολάκη* (Athens, N.D.). *Τυπικὸν τῆς 'Εκκλησιαστικῆς 'Ακολουθίας τῆς ἐν 'Ιεροσολύμοις 'Αγίας Λαύρας τοῦ 'Οσίου καὶ Θεοφόρου Πατρὸς ἡμῶν Σάββα,* "Εκδ. 'Ιεροδιακόνου Σπυρίδωνος Παπαδοπούλου (Venice, 1771).

[30]See Robert F. Taft, "Mt. Athos: A Late Chapter in the History of the Byzantine Rite," *Dumbarton Oaks Papers* (1988), pp. 179-194; "A Tale of Two Cities — The Byzantine Holy Week Tradition as a Paradigm of Liturgical History," in J. Neil Alexander, ed., *Time and Community* (Washington, 1990), pp. 21-41; and "In the Bridegroom's Absence. The Paschal Triduum in the Byzantine Church," in *Studia Anelmiana, Analecta Liturgica,* vol. 102 (1990), pp. 71-97. In this latter article Fr. Taft sums up the process of the development in these words, ". . . as the rite of Constantinople is being monas-

ticized via Palestine, the rite of Palestine is being further byzantinized. The ultimate result of this evolution is the hybrid new-Sabaitic synthesis we know as the 'Byzantine Rite' " (p. 73). Gabriel Bertoniere, "The Historical Development of the Easter Vigil and Related Services in the Greek Church," *Orientalia Christiana Analecta* 193 (Rome, 1972).

[31]See "The Liturgy of the Great Church" in *Dumbarton Oaks Papers* 34-35 (1980-81).

[32]See the notable work of Juan Mateos, *Le Typicon de la Grande Église,* vols. 1, 2 (Rome, 1962, 1963). These volumes contain a critical text of the Typikon, with an introduction and a French translation. See also, Evangelos Antoniades, "Περὶ τοῦ Ἀσματικοῦ ἢ Βυζαντινοῦ Κοσμικοῦ Τύπου τῶν Ἀκολουθιῶν τῆς Ἡμερονυκτίου Προσευχῆ," *Θεολογία* 21-22 (1949-51). It is of interest to note, that, in our own time, the Monastery of New Skete (OCA) in Cambridge, NY, has used elements of the Cathedral Office in forming its own typikon. The Monastery has published a series of handsome volumes, that reflect its liturgical practice and usage. For a discussion on the liturgical practices of New Skete, and a longer bibliography on the Cathedral Office of Constantinople, see Robert Taft, "The Byzantine Office in the Prayerbook of New Skete: Evaluation of Proposed Reform," *Orientalia Christiana Periodica* 48 (1982) 336-370.

[33]See A. Calivas, Χρόνος Τελέσεως τῆς Θείας Λειτουργίας, pp. 36-41.

[34]See *Festal Menaion*, p. 543.

[35]The decision to revise the Typikon is especially significant for our times. It constitutes the basis, as well as the supporting argument for the continued review and study of our liturgical practices. Liturgical reform based on sound theological, devotional, spiritual and historical principles helps sustain the dynamic character of worship and provides the possibilities for creative continuity.

[36]Ἡ Ἁγία καὶ Μεγάλη Ἑβδομάς (Constantinople, 1906).

[37]Ἀκολουθία Κατανυκτικὴ τῆς Ἁγίας καὶ Μεγάλης Τεσσαρακοστῆς ἀπὸ τῆς Κυριακῆς τῆς Τυρινῆς Ἑσπέρας Μέχρι τῆς Κυριακῆς τοῦ Πάσχα (Athens, 1895). The notes of the editor are especially useful for the study of the liturgical practices in the last century.

[38]The ninth edition was published in 1985 under the supervision of Protopresbyter Konstantinos Papagiannis. Also, the Apostolike Diakonia has published "pocket-size" versions of the text for use by the laity. Other publishing houses in Greece also have printed the Patriarchal Text.

[39]To my knowledge, the classical work of John Glenn King, *The Rites and Ceremonies of the Greek Church, in Russia* (1772), was the first English translation of Orthodox liturgical texts.

[40]At one time the Liturgy of the Pre-sanctified Gifts was celebrated on Great Friday. The practice ceased long ago, probably for reasons of practicality due to the length of the divine services assigned to the day.

[41]For reasons noted below these vesperal liturgies have been transposed to the morning hours of Great Thursday and Great Saturday.

[42]The text for this service is found in the Εὐχολόγιον. It is contained also in the Holy Week Book, edited by Father G. Papadeas.

[43]The text for this service is not contained in the published editions of the Triodion. It is found in special volumnes published by the Patriarchate of Jerusalem and the Monastery of St. John the Theologian at Patmos.

[44]P. 243.

[45]Τυπικὸν τῆς τοῦ Χριστοῦ Μεγάλης Ἐκκλησίας, p. 362, note 46.

[46]Χριστιανικὴ Ἠθικὴ καὶ Λειτουργική, p. 243. Cf. Typikon, p. 355, note 42, and p. 301,

note 51. I. Fountoules Ἀπαντήσεις,vol. 2 (Thessalonike, 1975), p. 209 ff.

[47]Τυπικόν, p. 362. a. careful study of the development of the horarium of the divine services in both the cathedral and monastic offices would prove useful in understanding, at least in part, these gradual shifts. What exactly were the assigned and actual hours of the daily office in the monasteries and the secular churches during the early and late medieval periods? How was the ordering of the horaria affected by the revisions or replacement of the Typika? What changes in societal structures affected the Church and impacted on the horaria? I have argued elsewhere, e.g., that such changes during the course of the early centuries brought about the transfer of the original evening eucharistic assembly first to the pre-dawn hours and later to the "third" hour of the day (see, Χρόνος Τελέσεως, pp. 165-96). Another item that may shed some light on the transposition of the Paschal Vigil Liturgy is related to the rule that allows for the celebration of only one Divine Liturgy by one priest on one altar on a given day or feast. Could a strict interpretation of this rule also have contributed to the shift of the Pachal Vigil Liturgy?

[48]See Robert Taft, *The Liturgy of the Hours in East and West* (Collegeville, 1986), pp. 165-90.

[49]See below, Chapter Four, Great Friday. Also, in the tradition of Jerusalem the Orthros of Great Saturday was celebrated as a nocturnal celebration.

[50]The only service conducted at the regularly appointed hour is the Vesper Service of Great Friday.

[51]See Mateos, *Le Typicon*, pp. 72-78.

[52]Thomas Merton, *Seasons of Celebration* (New York, 1977), p. 148.

[53]See Raymond E. Brown, *An Adult Christ at Christmas* (The Liturgical Press, 1987), p. 9.

[54]For an excellent concise commentary on the themes of Great Week and Pascha, see *The Year of Grace*, by a Monk of the Eastern Church (Crestwood, 1980), pp. 135-81. See also, *The Lenten Triodion*, pp. 57-64.

[55]E.g. "Today Bethany proclaims beforehand the Resurrection of Christ the Giver of Life, and it rejoices at the rising of Lazaros" (Orthros, First Ode hymn). The translations of the hymns cited are from *The Lenten Triodion*.

[56]E.g. "Giving us before the Passion an assurance of the general resurrection, Thou hast raised Lazaros from the dead, O Christ our God . . ." (Apolytikion).

[57]E.g., "O Lord, Thou has said to Martha, 'I am the Resurrection'; and Thou hast confirmed Thy words by actions calling Lazaros from hades . . ." (Orthros, a hymn of the Ainoi). "Christ, the joy of all, the truth, the light, the life, the resurrection of the world, in His love appeared to those on earth; and He became Himself the pattern of our resurrection, granting divine forgiveness unto all" (Kontakion).

[58]E.g. "O Lord, taking Thy disciples, Thou hast come to Bethany to awaken Lazaros. Weeping for him in accordance with the law of human nature, Thou hast as God raised up the four-day corpse, and he cried out to Thee, our Saviour: 'O Blessed Lord, glory to Thee' " (A hymn of Vespers).

[59]Veselin Kesich, *The Gospel Image of Christ* (Crestwood, 1972), p. 110.

[60]See *The Art of Prayer — An Orthodox Anthology* (London, 1985), pp. 180-81.

[61]See, Serge S. Verhovsky, *The Light of the World* (Crestwood, 1982), pp. 93-96.

[62]Veselin Kesich, *The Gospel Image*, p. 97.

[63]The fourth century nun, Egeria, who travelled extensively in the East describes the custom as she observed it in Jerusalem towards the end of the fourth century: "As the eleventh hour draws near, that particular passage from Scripture is read in which the

children bearing palms and branches came forth to meet the Lord, saying: Blessed is
He who comes in the name of the Lord. The bishop and all the people rise immediately, and then everyone walks down from the top of the Mount of Olives, with the people
preceding the bishop and responding continually with 'Blessed is He who comes in
the name of the Lord' to the hymns and antiphons. All the children who are present
here, including those who are not yet able to walk because they are too young and
therefore are carried on their parents' shoulders, all of them bear branches, some carrying palms, others, olive branches. And the bishop is led in the same manner as the
Lord once was led. From the top of the mountain as far as the city, and from there
through the entire city as far as the Anastasis, everyone accompanies the bishop the
whole way on foot, and this includes distinguished ladies and men of consequence,
reciting the responses all the while; and they move very slowly so that the people will
not tire." *Egeria: Diary of a Pilgrimage*, Ancient Christian Writers, no. 38 (Trans. G. E.
Gingras), chapters 30, 31.

[64]Icons play an important role in the worship of the Church. Persons and events of
sacred history are depicted mystically and embodied liturgically. The icon brings before
us the transfigured world. According to St. John of Damascus, "they make things so
obviously manifest, enabling us to perceive hidden things" (*On the Divine Images*, 3,
17). In the course of Great Week the Church displays several different icons related
to the specific liturgical observance. The main icons of Great Week are the following:
The Raising of Lazaros; The Triumphant Entry ('Η Βαϊφόρος); The Nymphios; The
Mystical Supper ('Ο Μυστικὸς Δεῖπνος); The Crucifixion; The Extreme Humility (Η ῎Ακρα
Ταπείνωσις); The Epitaphios (Burial); and The Descent into Hades ('Η εἰς ῎Αδου Κάθοδος),
which expresses in visible form the truths resulting from Christ's resurrection.

[65]The ordinary liturgical Trisagion is replaced by the Baptismal Trisagion ("As many
as have been baptized into Christ have put on Christ. Alleluia" Gal 3.27). The Baptismal Trisagion is used at all the great feasts of the Church, because it was the custom
to baptize catechumens at these festivals.

The Typikon of the Great Church (ca. 10 century) indicates that at Constantinople
on the Saturday of Lazaros the Patriarch administered baptism in the small baptistery
of Hagia Sophia (see Juan Mateos, *Le Typicon de la Grande* Église, p. 62). The reason
for conducting baptisms on this day is unclear; especially since the Patriarch also administered baptism one week later, on Great Saturday evening in the great baptistry
(ibid. p. 84). It has been suggested that the practice of baptizing on the Saturday of
Lazaros came to Constantinople from Alexandria. There, in accordance to two primitive
traditions, the baptism of the catechumens at the end of the Fast was associated with
two events in the life of Jesus. The first held that the day Jesus "conferred" baptism
(Jn 3.22; 4.2) coincides with the end of the Church's forty day fast. The second is related
to the so called "secret Gospel of Mark," i.e., a pericope in which the Evangelist re-
counts the raising of an unnamed youth at Bethany. The passage, which corresponds
to the event described in the Gospel in John, has baptismal motifs and reportedly was
read to those preparing to receive baptism. Thus, we find at least a tentative connection for the practice of baptizing on the Saturday of Lazaros. [See Thomas J. Talley,
The Origins of the Liturgical Year (New York, 1986), pp. 203-14.]

For additional information on the use of the ordinary and special liturgical Trisagia,
see Demetri Conomos, *Byzantine Trisagia and Cherubika*, (Thessalonike, 1974).

[66]The Communion Hymn (Κοινωνικόν) is sung while the clergy and laity receive Holy Communion. The custom to accompany the act of Communion with psalmody is an
ancient liturgical practice. A whole psalm or a portion of it was usually employed as
the hymn. Early sources point to the use of Psalms 33 (34) and 144 (145) as ancient
Communion hymns. Initially, the hymn was used to draw the attention of the faithful

to the Sacrament. Eventually, a cycle of hymns was developed, each assigned to one or more occasions in the liturgical year. In this second stage of development, the selection of the hymn helped to highlight the meaning of a particular feast. Thus, the Communion hymn serves two main purposes: to direct the attention of the faithful to the divine mystery of Communion, as well as to remind them of the meaning of the feast being observed. The Communion hymn for the Saturday of Lazaros is taken from Psalm 8.3. For a comprehensive study on the Communion hymn, see Dimitri E. Conomos, *The Late Byzantine and Slavonic Communion Cycle: Liturgy and Music* (Dumbarton Oaks Research Library and Collection, 1985).

[67]The second apolytikion contains baptismal imagery and is related to the medieval practice mentioned above concerning the administration of baptism at the end of the Fast.

[68]See J. Mateos, "Quelques Problèmes de l'Orthros Byzantine," *Proche Orient Chrétien* 11 (1961) 17-35, 201-20. Robert Taft, *The Liturgy of the Hours in East and West* (Collegeville, 1986), pp. 191-213 and 273-91. B. D. Stuhlman, "The Morning Offices of the Byzantine Rite: Mateos Revisited," *Studia Liturgica*, 19 (1984) 162-73.

[69]See Georges Barrois, *Scripture Readings in Orthodox Worship* (Crestwood, 1977), p. 142.

[70]Demetrios Trakatellis, *Authority and Passion* (Brookline, 1987), p. 82.

[71]A product of spiritual sterility, false religiosity leads to arrogance, self-righteousness and hypocrisy. It causes hearts to harden with envy, intolerance, fanaticism and hatred. It misuses and misappropriates worship, man's most profound and sublime activity, reducing it to empty, ostentatious and hypocritical expressions of piety.

[72]Nicholas Cabasilas, *The Life in Christ* (Crestwood, 1974), pp. 57-60.

[73]*The Living God: A Catechism for the Christian Faith* 1 (Crestwood, 1989), pp. 190-91.

[74]Kallistos Ware, *The Orthodox Way* (Crestwood, 1979), p. 180.

[75]John D. Zizioulas, "The Mystery of the Church in Orthodox Traditon," *One in Christ* 24/4 (1988) 294.

[76]This idea of progress is developed by Fr. Dumitru Staniloae, *Theology and the Church* (Crestwood, 1980), pp. 169-80.

[77]Ibid. pp. 172-73. Echoing St. Gregory of Nyssa, Bishop Kallistos describes this ἐπέκτασις or reaching forward with the following words: "Because God is infinite, this constant reaching forward proves limitless. The soul possesses God, and yet still seeks him; her joy is full, and yet grows always more intense. God grows ever nearer to us, yet he still remains the Other; we behold him face to face, yet we still continue to advance further and further into the divine mystery. Although strangers no longer, we do not cease to be pilgrims. We go forward 'from glory to glory' (2 Cor 3.18), and then to a glory that is greater still. Never, in all eternity, shall we reach a point we have accomplished all there is to do, or discovered all that there is to know," in *The Orthodox Way*, p. 185.

[78]*The Living God, A Catechism for the Christian Faith*, vol. 2, p. 337.

[79]Eds. G. Palmer, P. Sherrard, K. Ware, *The Philokalia* vol. 1 (London, 1979), pp. 164-65.

[80]Panayiotis Nellas, *Deification in Christ* (Crestwood, 1987), p. 30.

[81]Christos Yannaras, *The Freedom of Morality* (Crestwood, 1984), p. 33.

[82]*The Philokalia*, vol. 2, p. 181.

[83]The love of God for sinners is described by the following story told by the desert

fathers: "An old man was asked by a soldier, 'Does God accept repentance?' The reply 'Tell me, my dear, if your cloak is torn, do you throw it away?' Answering him, the soldier said, 'No, I mend it and use it again.' The old man said to him, 'If you spare your own vesture, would God not be kind to his own image?'" Quoted in Irenee Hausherr, *Spiritual Direction in the Early Christian East* (Kalamazoo, 1990), p. 253.

[84]See *The Philokalia*, vol. 2, p. 386.

[85]In one of his writings, St. John Chrysostom noted, "Did you commit sin? Enter the Church and repent for your sin; for here is the physician, not the judge; here one is not investigated, one receives remission of sins."

[86]This icon depicts Christ as He appeared before Pilate, wearing the crown of thorns and the purple robe. Pilate presented Him, saying "Behold the man — Ἰδοὺ ὁ ἄνθρωπος" (Jn 19.5). The Bridegroom is the Suffering Servant.

[87]The reason for censing at this time is probably related to an early liturgical practice, according to which the whole church was censed before the beginning of each service. By this act we signify the presence of the Holy Spirit in the midst of the liturgical assembly. This much is indicated by the prayer for the offering of the incence, "We offer You incense, Christ our God, as an offering of spiritual fragrance. Accept it before Your heavenly altar and send down upon us in return the grace of Your all Holy Spirit."

[88]The word "katzion" comes from the Italian "cazza," which means crucible. The early Church used stationary as well as portable censers or thuribles. In current liturgical practice we use two types of portable censers. In the usual form, the container is suspended on chains from which it is swung. In the second form, the container is held by a handle. It is waved rythmically by a twist of the wrist.

[89]For a discussion on the history, character and order of the Liturgy of the Pre-Sanctified Gifts see, Nicholas Uspensky, "The Liturgy of the Pre-Sanctified Gift — History and Practice" in Evening Worship in the Orthodox Church (Crestwood, 1985), pp. 111-90. Alexander Schmemann, *Great Lent* (Crestwood, 1974), pp. 45-61. D. Moraites, Ἡ Λειτουργία τῶν Προηγιασμένων (Thessalonike, 1955). Ioannis Fountoules, Λειτουργία Προηγιασμένων Δώρων — Κείμενα Λειτουργικῆς 8 (Thessalonike, 1971). A. Calivas, Χρόνος Τελέσεως τῆς Θείας Λειτουργίας, pp. 154-64; and Ἱεροτελεστικόν — Handbook of Rubrics (unpublished notes — Brookline, 1985). V. S. Janeras, "La partie vespérale de la Liturgie Byzantine des Présanctifies," *Orientalia Christiana Periodica* 30 (1964) 193-222.

[90]The Anaphora is the one indispensible element for the celebration of a full and complete Divine Liturgy. It is the great eucharistic prayer, whose component parts include: the introductory *dialogue*; the *thanksgiving* for God's mighty acts in creation and redemption; the *Trisagion*; the narrative of the *institution*; the *anamnesis*; the *epiclesis* which includes the invocation of the Holy Spirit, the consecration of the gifts and the statement concerning the fruits of communion; the *diptychs* which include the commemoration of the saints and the intercessory prayer for the dead and the living; and the concluding *doxology*. The Anaphora begins after the kiss of peace and the recitation of the Creed with the invitation "Let us lift up our hearts."

[91]St. Basil among others makes reference to this practice. He notes, ". . . it is superfluous to show that the act is no way offensive, since long continued custom has confirmed this practice . . . In fact, all the monks of the desert, where there is no priest, preserve holy Communion in their own house and receive it from their own hands. In Alexandria and Egypt each person, even those belonging to the laity, has Communion in his own home, and when he wishes he receives with his own hand. For, when the priest has once and for all completed the sacrifice and has given Communion, the recipient, participating in it each time daily as entire, is bound to believe that he properly

takes and receives it from the giver. Because in the Church also the priest gives out a portion, and the one who receives it holds it in all lawfullness, and in this way carries it by his own hand to his mouth. It is virtually the same whether he receives one particle from the priest or many particles at one time." *Epistle 93.* See *The Fathers of the Church — St. Basil's Letters,* vol. 1, pp. 208-09.

[92]See A. Calivas, Χρόνος Τελέσεως τῆς Θείας Λειτουργίας, pp. 158-63. C. M. Enisleidos, Ὁ Θεσμὸς τῆς Νηστείας (Athens, 1959), pp. 49-80 and 94-95.

[93]See A. Schmemann, *Great Lent,* p. 49.

[94]For more on the eucharistic fast see, A. Schmemann, *Great Lent,* pp. 45-55. Ioannis Fountoules, Λειτουργικὰ Θέματα, vol. 3 (Thessalonike, 1977), pp. 77-79. A. Calivas, Χρόνος Τελέσεως τῆς Θείας Λειτουργίας, pp. 188-90.

[95]Synod of Laodicea, Canons 49 and 51, Πηδάλιον, p. 438. G. Ralles and M. Potles, Σύνταγμα τῶν Θείων καὶ Ἱερῶν Κανόνων 3 (Athens, 1852), pp. 216, 218. Also, Synod of Troullo, Canon 52, Πηδάλιον, p. 267. G. Ralles and M. Potles, Σύνταγμα, vol. 2, p. 427.

[96]A. Schmemann, *Great Lent,* p. 47.

[97]See Πασχάλιον Χρονικόν, PG 92.989B. Patriarch Nikephoros of Constantinople (805-815) informs us of this practice as well. Cited in D. Moraites, Ἡ Λειτουργία τῶν Προηγιασμένων, p. 30. See also J. Mateos, *Le Typicon de la Grande Église,* 2, pp. 82 and 188. It is important to note that at one point in time the marriage rite also was conducted within the context of a Pre-Sanctified Liturgy. See, P. N. Trembelas, Μικρὸν Εὐχολόγιον, vol. 1, pp. 15-17, 62, 66.

[98]Cyril of Alexandria, commenting on the reserved sacrament, noted the following: "I hear that some people say that the mystical blessing is no longer active to effect sanctification when the Eucharist is left over to the next day. Those who reason this way are insane. For Christ does not become different, and His holy Body does not undergo any change. On the contrary, the effectiveness of the life-creating grace in It remains unchanged." *Epistle to Calosirius* in PG 76.1073-76. Cited in N. Uspensky, *Evening Worship,* p. 154.

[99]For a full discussion on the Sacrament of Holy Unction see, M. J. O'Connell, trans., *Temple of the Holy Spirit — Sickness and Death of the Christian in the Liturgy* (Pueblo, 1983). Stanley S. Harakas, *Health and Medicine in the Eastern Orthodox Tradition* (Crossroad, 1990). A. Calivas, "The Mystery of Holy Unction" in *A Companion to the Greek Orthodox Church* 2nd Edition (New York, 1988). *The Living God — A Catechism,* 2 (Crestwood, 1988), pp. 327-30. Paul Meyendorff, "The Anointing of the Sick: Some Pastoral Considerations," SVTQ 35/2-3 (1991) 241-55. Ioannis Fountoules, Ἀκολουθία τοῦ Εὐχελαίου (Thessalonike, 1978). P. N. Trembelas, Μικρὸν Εὐχολόγιον, 1 (Athens, 1950), pp. 99-191.

[100]*The Living God,* p. 329.

[101]In European countries, for example, the communal service of Holy Unction is usually celebrated in the afternoon of Great Wednesday.

[102]For a description of the service and the rubrics see, A. Calivas, Ἱεροτελεστικόν.

[103]The Orthros service begins with a brief office for those in authority. The office was probably celebrated in monasteries established by emperors. Gradually, it became a permanent element of the Orthros. In parish usuage, however, the Royal Psalms fell into disuse long ago, except during Great Week, when the old practice is retained. The royal troparia, however, continue to be used at all Orthros services.

[104]Properly, the prayer "Heavenly King" is said at the beginning of the Midnight Service which precedes the Orthros. However, it is now common practice to recite it at this point, especially since the Midnight Service is suppressed in parish usage.

[105]See above, notes 87 and 88.

[106]The Psalms play an important role in the worship of the Orthodox Church. One may even say that the Psalter is the most beloved and most used prayer book of the Church. Some of the psalms or groups of psalms have acquired technical names by which they are easily identified. The Hexapsalmos (Ἑξάψαλμος) is one such name. It identifies the set of six (ἕξ) psalms that are read at every Orthros service (Pss 3, 37, 62, 87, 102 and 142). Other important titles of psalms include the following: Ainoi — Αἶνοι or Praises (Pss 148, 149, 150); Amomos — Ἄμωμος (Ps. 118); Antiphons: set of Psalms with refrains and priestly prayers; Polyeleos — Πολυέλεος (Pss 134, 135); Pro-oimiakos — Προοιμιακός (Ps 103); Proskyrion — Προσκύριον (Pss 119-133); Tripsalmos — Τρίψαλμος (the sets of three Psalms read at each service of the Hours); and Typika — Τυπικά: Pss 102, 145, and the Beatitudes. It should be noted that we are using the Septuagint number of the Psalms.

[107]The procession begins in the sanctuary; it procedes out through the north door of the Iconostasion, up the north aisle and down the south aisle of the Church, and concludes at the solea. The icon is placed on a stand (προσκυνητάριον) in the middle of the solea. Care is taken to decorate the icon with appropriate flowers before the service. The acolytes and chanters precede the priest, as per the usual order. We may be reminded at this point that in accordance with the ancient tradition of the rite of Constantinople, the processional cross is carried at the head of the procession. The procession of the icon of the Nymphios is a relatively new development. It began to appear in the last century, probably in imitation of the procession of the Ἐσταυρωμένος on Great Thursday.

[108]One of the important liturgical books of the Orthodox Church is the Psalter (Ψαλτήριον). It contains the 150 Psalms of the Old Testament. Many printed editions of the Psalter include the nine Odes of the Old and New Testaments, that form the basis of the Canon of the Orthros Services.

In accordance to ancient monastic practices and customs, the Psalter is divided into twenty sections of approximately equal length. These sections are called Kathismata [Κάθισμα (s.); Καθίσματα (pl.)]. Each Kathisma is sub-divided into three sub-sections or "staseis" (στάσεις). The Kathismata of the Psalter are recited according to a specified arrangement in the Orthros and Vesper services. In monasteries the Psalter continues to be recited fully once each week. During Great Week the complete Psalter is read in the first three days. This arrangement of the Psalter has come to us from the Palestinian urban monastic tradition. The psalter of the now defunct Cathedral Office (the asmatike akolouthia — sung office) was arranged differently. Besides the differences in arrangement, the two psalters also differed in the manner in which they were recited. The psalter of Constantinople presupposed an antiphonal recitation of the Psalms with a refrain at each verse. The Palestinian psalter is recited by a soloist without response. [For a description on the use of Psalms in the Orthodox liturgical tradition see J. A. Lamb, *The Psalms in Christian Worship* (London, 1962).]

[109]If two or more priests are co-celebrating, the Gospel at the Orthros service is read by the senior priest.

[110]Though this has become the prevailing practice, I do not believe it is improper for the priest to read the Gospel from the pulpit. (Of course, there is one exception. The regular Sunday morning Gospel [Ἑωθινόν] is always read at the right side of the Holy Table).

[111]The word 'exaposteilarion' comes from the verb ἐξαποστέλλω — to send forth. In some services these hymns are known as photagogika — φωταγωγικά. They are called this because Christ is implored to send forth His light.

By custom the Bishop and/or Priest reverence the icon of the Nymphios when the Exaposteilarion is being sung. In some traditions the faithful do so also. Where this practice is followed, it is important that proper order and decorum be observed.

[112]The Doxastikon is the last hymn of the series. It is called by that name because it is preceded by the phrase "Δόξα Πατρὶ καὶ Υἱῷ καὶ 'Αγίῳ Πνεύματι . . . — Glory to the Father," etc. If a Theotokion is to follow, then the concluding part of the phrase, "Καὶ νῦν . . . — Both now and forever" is placed before the Theotokion hymn. In our liturgical tradition any group or series of Psalms is concluded by the doxological phrase "Glory to the Father . . ."

[113]The Small Doxology, unlike the Great Doxology, is recited and not sung. Also, it is introduced by a brief doxology to the Holy Trinity, and it does not conclude with the Trisagion.

[114]At some point before the Apolysis the priest should preach the Word of God. It would be best if the sermon were to follow the Gospel. The priest should not neglect this important ministry or underestimate its value.

[115]Many books and articles have been written recently about the Eucharist and the Divine Liturgy. Among them are some of the following: A. Schmemann, *The Eucharist* (Crestwood, 1988). Hugh Wybrew, *The Orthodox Liturgy* (Crestwood, 1990). H. J. Schultz, *The Byzantine Liturgy* (New York, 1986). S. Harakas, *Living the Liturgy* (Minneapolis, 1974). T. Stylianopoulos, *The Eternal Liturgy* (Brookline, 1987). E. Clapsis, "The Eucharist as Missionary Event in a Suffering World," in G. Lemopoulos, ed. *Your Will Be Done* (Geneva, 1989), pp. 161-71. A. Calivas, "An Introduction to the Divine Liturgy" in *The Divine Liturgy of St. John Chrysostom* (Brookline, 1985); and "The Eucharist: The Sacrament of the Economy of Salvation" in Ben F. Meyer, ed., *One Loaf, One Cup* (in publication).

[116]See J. D. Zizioulas, *Being as Communion* (Crestwood, 1985) pp. 78-82.

[117]Jn 3.3-6; Rom 6.3-12; Eph 4.22-24; Col 3.1-10.

[118]See the Prayer before the Lord's Prayer, Divine Liturgy of St. James (Iakovos).

[119]This need for spiritual discernment was addressed by St. Paul (1 Cor 11.29). Similar admonitions are found in the writings of the Fathers and are embedded in the texts of the Divine Liturgy itself. Two such warnings are part of the invitation to Holy Communion: "The Holy Gifts for the Holy People of God," and "Approach with the fear of God, with faith and with love." Sanctification is a fruit of Communion and not the precondition for its reception. This idea is clearly stated by Nicholas Cabasilas: "Let not everyone come to receive it, but only those who are worthy, 'for the holy gifts are for the holy people of God.' Those whom the priest calls holy are not only those who have attained perfection, but also those who are striving for it without having yet obtained it . . . That is why Christians, if they have not committed such sins (mortal sins) as would cut them off from Christ and bring death, are in no way prevented, when partaking of the holy mysteries, from receiving sanctification . . . For no one has holiness of himself; it is not the consequence of human virtue, but comes for all from Him and through Him." *A Commentary on the Divine Liturgy* 36; PG 150.448-49.

[120]The Anaphora of the Divine Liturgy of St. John Chrysostom.

[121]Homily 56. Quoted in J. Meyendorff, *A Study of Gregory Palamas* (London, 1964) p. 177. See also Georgios Mantzarides, *The Deification of Man* (Crestwood, 1984) p. 53.

[122]A Monk of the Eastern Church, *Serve the Lord with Gladness* (Crestwood, 1990) pp. 81-85.

[123]Demetrios Trakatellis, *Authority and Passion* (Brookline, 1987), p. 96.

[124]*The Apostolic Tradition of Hippolytus*, trans. B. S. Easton (Ann Arbor, 1962), p. 56.

[125]The portion of the bread concecrated to become the Body of Christ and distributed as Holy Communion at the Eucharist is called "The Lamb." John the Baptist identified Jesus as the Lamb of God. The title has clear sacrificial connotations (Is 53.2-7 and Acts 8.32-35). The reason for preparing two Lambs is obvious. The one is for communion at the Divine Liturgy, while the other is reserved.

[126]Where the Sacrament of Unction is conducted on the afternoon of Great Wednesday, the Orthros of Great Thursday is chanted in the evening in accordance with the order in the Triodion. At the Chapel of the Holy Cross, it is celebrated after the Service of the Euchelaion on Great Wednesday evening.

[127]See the rubrics in the defunct Typicon of the Great Church, Mateos, *Le Typicon de la Grande Église*, pp. 72-76. The rubrics of this Typicon tell us that the Holy Table was also washed on Great Thursday afternoon.

[128]It should be noted that this Gospel pericope is a compilation of several texts, even though it is attributed to the Evangelist Matthew. Such a liturgical practice was not uncommon in antiquity. It is an attempt to draw together all the elements of a particular event. This pericope is the longest Gospel reading at a Divine Liturgy.

[129]The hymns sung at the Great Entrance are known as the Cherubikon. They are called by this name because the ordinary or most common of these hymns begins with the words "Οἱ τὰ Χερουβίμ — We who mystically represent the Cherubim."

On Great Thursday the ordinary hymn is replaced by another, more appropriate to the commemoration of the institution of the Eucharist at the Mystical Supper. It is the hymn "Τοῦ Δείπνου σου τοῦ Μυστικοῦ — Of Your Mystical Supper . . ." It is said that the hymn was first used as a substitute Cherubikon in the latter part of the sixth century. The hymn is sung regularly as a Communion hymn. For a detailed study on the repertory of Cherubic hymns see, Dimitri E. Conomos, *Byzantine Trisagia and Cherubika* (Thessalonike, 1974).

[130]Boris Bobrinskoy, "Old Age and Death: Tragedy or Blessing," SVTQ 28/4 (1984) 242.

[131]The Pre-Sanctified Liturgy was added to the Vespers on Great Friday. See J. Mateos, *Le Typicon*, pp. 80-82. The Divine Liturgy we now celebrate on Great Saturday morning belongs to the liturgical cycle of Pascha and not Great Week, as we shall see below.

[132]The nucleus of this service was formed in Jerusalem during the fourth century. Subsequent developments occurred in stages through the synthesis of elements from the liturgical practices and traditions of the Cathedral and monastic offices of both Jerusalem and Constantinople. For a thorough analysis of the history and development of the divine services of Great Friday, see the excellent study of Sebastia Janeras, *Le Vendredi-Saint dans La Tradition Liturgique Byzantine* (Studia Anselmiana 99), (Analecta Liturgica 12), (Rome, 1988). See also, Robert Taft, "A Tale of Two Cities: The Byzantine Holy Week Triduum as a Paradigm of Liturgical History" in *Time and Community*, ed. J. N. Alexander (Washington, D.C., 1990), pp. 21-41, and "In the Bridegroom's Absence," *Analecta Liturgica*, pp. 71-97.

[133]The series of the twelve Passion lections was constructed in Constantinople during the ninth century by merging two Jerusalem cycles, the lections of the vigil conducted on Great Thursday night and the Great Friday day services. From the descriptions of the solemnities of Great Thursday and Great Friday provided in the Diary of Egeria, we know that Jerusalem already had a well developed series of Passion lections as early as the fourth century. Two other ancient documents, the Armenian Lectionary (417-439 A.D.) and the Georgian Lectionary (5th-8th c.), provide us with additional information about the liturgical practices and developments of the Jerusalem Church

from the fifth to the eighth centuries. More specifically, on the topic of the lections under consideration, the Armenian Lectionary contains seven Passion lections, while the later Georgian Lectionary lists eight such pericopes. These lists were reworked in Constantinople, which produced an augmented series of eleven and later twelve Passion lections, the same as those found in the present service of the Great Friday Orthros.

Janeras has suggested that the increased number of eleven lections was devised to parallel the eleven pericopes commemorating the Resurrection, which form part of the Sunday Orthros and are read in a recurring cycle of eleven weeks, beginning with the Sunday after Pentecost and ending on the Fifth Sunday of the Great Lent.

The augmented series of the Passion readings was introduced into Jerusalem. There it passed into the new Sabaite Typikon to become part of the Great Friday Orthros we know today.

Originally, the Great Friday solemnities at Constantinople were simpler than those of Jerusalem. According to the Typikon of the Great Church (10th c.), the services assigned to Great Friday were as follows: the Pannychis, celebrated at the conclusion of the divine services of Great Thursday; the Orthros and the Trithekte on Great Friday morning; and the Vespers with the Pre-Sanctified Liturgy on Great Friday evening. In addition, the Patriarch conducted the pre-baptismal rites in the Church of Hagia Eirene, while the relic of the sacred Lance (Λόγχη) was displayed for veneration at Hagia Sophia.

The Passion readings in the Cathedral Office of Constantinople were centered originally in the Vesperal Liturgy of Great Thursday and the Vespers of Great Friday. No Passion lections were assigned to the Orthros or the Trithekte of Great Friday. However, after its development in the ninth century, Constantinople assigned the augmented series of twelve Passion lections to the Pannychis. The Typikon of the Great Church (10th c.) lists these readings in the Pannychis, a service described as "Παννυχὶς τῶν Παθῶν τοῦ Κυρίου ἡμῶν Ἰησοῦ Χριστοῦ" or "The Pannychis of the Passion of our Lord Jesus Christ" (J. Mateos, *Le Typicon*, pp. 76-78).

From the information gleaned from these ancient sources, it becomes apparent that the early liturgical celebrations of the Passion were essentially nocturnal, conducted in the context of a vigil. This fact remained operative, even when the liturgical units began to break down. Thus, the Great Friday Orthros, with its series of twelve Passion lections continues to be celebrated on Great Thursday night as a type of vigil.

On a different note, the reform of the lectionary of Great Friday — as with the reform of the lectionary in general — is not a matter of simply shortening some readings or omitting or adding others. The issue is far more complex. Any discussion on the reform of the lectionary must first take into account the matter of organizational principles. (See R. Taft, "In the Bridegroom's Absence," pp. 91-93.

[134]The story of the Lord's agony in the Garden is omitted from these narratives. It is included, however, in the Gospel read at the Divine Liturgy on Great Thursday and is one of the four commemorations of Great Thursday.

[135]The name derives from the movable icon depicting the crucified victorious Christ which is attached to it. The movable icon is a relatively new feature. The earlier tradition depicted the figure directly upon the wood.

[136]See, Violakis, *Typikon*, p. 404, note 1. This rite is not contained in the ancient Typika; and is not observed by the Slavic churches or by most monasteries. In some monasteries, the Cross is carried out and attached to a table during the Ninth Hour. The Epitaphios is placed on the table at a later service.

[137]See, *Egeria*, ch. 37: " . . . A throne is set up for the bishop on Golgotha behind the Cross, which now stands there. The bishop sits on his throne, a table covered with a linen cloth is set before him, and the deacons stand around the table. The gilded

silver casket containing the sacred wood of the cross is brought in and opened. Both the wood of the cross and the inscription are taken out and placed on the table. As soon as they have been placed on the table, the bishop, remaining seated, grips the ends of the sacred wood with his hands, while the deacons, who are standing about, keep watch over it. There is a reason why it is guarded in this manner. It is the practice here for all the people to come forth one by one, the faithful as well as the catechumens. to bow down before the table, kiss the holy wood, and then move on. It is said that someone (I do not know when) took a bite and stole a piece of the holy cross. Therefore, it is now guarded by the deacons standing around, lest there be anyone who would dare come and do that again. All the people pass through one by one; all of them bow down, touching the cross and the inscription, first with their foreheads, then with their eyes; and, after kissing the cross, they move on.''

[138]Antiphons are a special feature of the defunct Cathedral Office of Constantinople.

[139]The Beatitudes are taken from Matthew 5.3-12. In addition to this service, the Beatitudes are found in the Orthros of Thursday of Fifth Week of Lent and in the longer version of the Funeral Service in the Great Euchologion (which parallels an Orthros service). In addition, the Beatitudes constitute the third psalm in the Service of the Typika. Also, the Beatitudes are inserted into the Ninth Hour during the Great Lent (See, S. Janeras, *Le Vendredi-Saint*, pp. 164-71).

[140]Of particular interest are the series of the three idiomela troparia of each Hour. The earliest mention of the troparia is found in the Georgian Lectionary. Most ancient witnesses attribute their authorship to Sophronios of Jerusalem.

[141]This particular arrangement of three lections — Prophecy, Epistle, Gospel — is representative of the Cathedral Office of Constantinople. On occasion the Old Testament readings are increased in number.

[142]In addition to Great Friday, the liturgical books contain a service of The Great Hours for Christmas and Theophany. Some early manuscripts also contain a Service of The Great Hours for Great Thursday and Great Saturday. In the sixteenth century an attempt was made to introduce similar services for the Feast of Pentecost.

[143]The Great Hours of Christmas and Theophany are found in the Menaia of December and January respectively.

[144]The First Hour was the last service to be developed. From the beginning it was considered as an extension of the Orthros.

[145]The service is conducted around three o'clock. In some localities, however, it is celebrated earlier because of special needs and considerations. The 1888 Typikon places the service in the morning hours.

[146]These earlier rites are still practiced in Slavic churches and many monasteries.

[147]I have read that in some isolated instances in Greece a variation of the older practice persists. The large Cross is simply drapped with a linen cloth and brought into the sanctuary after the Gospel is read. The reason for this is that the Crucified figure of Christ is depicted directly upon the wood and is not, therefore, removable.

[148]The Epitaphios has its origins in the aer used in the procession of the Great Entrance at the Divine Liturgy. From an early date a large veil was carried in the procession and was used to cover the diskos and chalice. This veil was called νεφέλη or ἀήρ. Around the fourteenth century the veil began to take on a new form and was called Epitaphios. In this new form the cloth was embroidered, bearing at first an icon of the dead body of Christ. Gradually the icon became more complex, evolving finally to its present form depicting the "threnos" or "lamentation," which includes the figures of the Theotokos, Joseph of Arimathea, Nikodemos, the Myrrh-bearers, and Angels.

In a final stage of development the use of the Epitaphios was restricted to Great Week and the season of Pascha. The aer once again became a simple veil. The threnos came to be depicted upon the antimension as well. For additional information see, Robert Taft, *The Great Entrance*, pp. 216-19. See also P. Johnstone, *The Byzantine Tradition in Church Embroidery* (London, 1967). G. A. Soteriou, *Τὰ Λειτουργικὰ "Αμφια τῆς 'Ορθοδόξου 'Εκκλησίας* (Athens, 1949). For the origins of the processions of the Epitaphios see below, notes 183-87.

[149]See the *Lenten Triodion*, Great Friday Vespers, p. 616.

[150]This elaborate way of holding and processing with the Epitaphios is first mentioned in a Russian manuscript of the sixteenth century. The first Greek source to cite this practice is the 1838 Typikon of Constantine the Protopsaltis.

[151]It was the custom to carry the Epitaphios at the Great Entrance of the Divine Liturgy. This practice constitutes the source for the ritual of Great Friday.

[152]The custom of placing candles on the Cross is very old. In the Cathedral Office of Constantinople a processional cross, with three candles (one on each end of the horizontal bar and one on the vertical bar) was carried at the head of the various liturgical processions.

[153]This particular pericope is made up the following passages Mt 27.1-38; Lk 23.39-43; Mt 27.39-54; Jn 19.31-37; and Mt 27.55-61. Such composite pericopes are not unfamiliar to ancient practices and to our liturgical tradition. Their purpose is to present events and/or teachings in the fullest and clearest way possible. For additional information on the use of Scripture in our liturgical tradition see the informative study of Georges Barrois, *Scripture Readings in Orthodox Worship* (Crestwood, 1977). Of particular interest is the section devoted to Great Week and Pascha, pp. 71-106.

[154]After the service, the Estavromenos wrapped in the linen cloth is removed from the Holy Table. By custom, it is kept in the sanctuary or the vestry in a proper place. The Estavromenos is replaced on the Cross after the Apodosis of Pascha before the Vesper service of the feast of the Ascension.

[155]The Epitaphios is preceded by the choirs, cross, candles, exapteryga, censer, et al.

[156]The Kouvouklion represents the Tomb of Christ. It is a table usually with a canopy. It is decorated with flowers. Many Churches have a beautifully carved wooden Kouvouklion.

[157]See the Anaphora of the Divine Liturgy of St. Basil.

[158]Boris Bobrinskoy, "Old Age and Death . . ." p. 242.

[159]Boris Bobrinskoy, p. 242.

[160]In earlier times this service was part of a vigil that began late on the night of Great Friday and ended in the predawn hours of Great Saturday.

[161]It was customary for the clergy to wear the full set of vestments particular to each rank at every corporate worship service. This practice, however, was gradually relaxed. Today, the full set of vestments is worn for: the Divine Liturgy (including the Proskomide); the Orthros of Great Saturday; the "Agape" Vespers of Pascha; and throughout the New Week (Διακαινίσιμος 'Εβδομάς).

[162]In Greek antiquity the word ἐγκώμιον was used to denote a laudatory ode to a conqueror.

[163]The term appears in thirteenth century manuscripts. See Σ. Εὐστρατιάδου, 'Ακολουθία τοῦ Μεγαλου Σαββάτου καὶ τὰ Μεγαλυνάρια τοῦ 'Επιταφίου (Νέα Σιών, 1938), σελ. 10-11. See also Ε. Γ. Παντελάκη, "Νέα 'Εγκώμια τοῦ 'Επιταφίου," *Θεολογία* 14 (1936) 225-50, 310-29. Ν. Β. Τομαδάκη, *Εἰσαγωγὴ εἰς τὴν Βυζαντινὴν Φιλολογίαν*, vol. 1 (1958) 216-19.

[164]For a comprehensive study on the liturgical use of the Amomos, see, Diane H. Touliatos-Banker, *The Byzantine Amomos Chant of the Fourteenth and Fifteenth Centuries*, Analecta Blatadon 46 (Thessalonike, 1984).

[165]According to a fifteenth century Typikon, it seems that it was a custom in some places to chant the Amomos together with an undefined number of interpolated verses on several occasions, including Great Saturday as well as on the Feasts of the Dormition of the Theotokos, the Beheading of St. John the Baptist, the Apostles, bishops, martyrs and righteous. See, Touliatos-Banker, *The Byzantine Amomos*, p. 200.

[166]See, E. Γ. Παντελάκη, ''Νέα 'Εγκώμια τοῦ 'Επιταφίου'' p. 225.

[167]The term ῎Αμωμος — Amomos (blameless) comes from the first words of Ps 118 (119), ''Μακάριοι οἱ ἄμωμοι ἐν ὁδῷ — Blessed are those whose way is blameless.''

[168]The Amomos also forms part of the weekday Midnight Office, the Funeral Service, and the Services of the Small and Great Schema (monastic tonsure).

[169]See *Τυπικὸν τῆς τοῦ Χριστοῦ Μεγάλης 'Εκκλησίας*,'' pp. 362, 426. See also, 'Εμμανουὴλ Λιοδοπούλου, *'Ακολουθία Κατανυκτικὴ τῆς 'Αγίας καὶ Μεγάλης Τεσσαρακοστῆς* (Athens, 1895) p. 496.

[170]The same practical pastoral considerations probably prompted the shifting of the Morning Gospel in the Sunday Orthros to a later time in the service. In the order of the Orthros service, the Gospel is read before the Canon. However, both of the new Typika of 1838 and 1888 formalized the practice of reading the Sunday morning Gospel after the Eighth Ode of the Canon. Here too, there is a discrepancy between the liturgical books and the prevailing practice of the Greek Church.

[171]Because the Amomos was no longer sung at the Orthros of Great Saturday, it appears that an intermediate service of sorts was created at which the Amomos was recited and twelve of the fifteen Old Testament pericopes of the Paschal Vigil, also suppressed, were read. This ''intermediate session'' was conducted prior to the celebration of the Orthros or earlier before the Vespers, as noted in the Typikon of Violakis (p. 362) and the Patriarchal Text. As noted below, the Paschal Vesper Service contains a total of fifteen Old Testament lections. Of these only three have remained in use (the first, fourth and fifteenth). The other twelve have been suppressed. The reading of these twelve lections together with the Amomos constituted the content of the service noted in the Typikon of Violakis.

[172]The full set of Encomia contained in the prevailing liturgical texts are distributed as follows: seventy five in the First Stasis; sixty two in the Second; and forty eight in the Third.

[173]See 'Η 'Αγία καὶ Μεγάλη 'Εβδομάς,'' 9th edition, 1985, pp. 14-16.

[174]This collection was formed by the late Emmanuel Farlekas, the well-known author and student of ritual rubrics. See, 'Η 'Αγία καὶ Μεγάλη 'Εβδομάς, pp. 15, 294-312.

[175]The services in this book are ''according to the use of the Orthodox Greek Church in London'' (title page). This book lists eight verses for the First stasis; nine for the second; and seventeen for the third.

[176]The Papadeas edition has the following distribution: 18, 13, and 31.

[177]The O Logos collection has 15, 13, and 26.

[178]Each Kathisma of the Psalter read at the Orthros is followed by a set of sessional hymns. The Evlogetaria hymns are called thusly, because they are introduced by the twelfth verse of the Amomos (Ps. 118). The verse begins with the word Εὐλογητός — Blessed (''Εὐλογητὸς εἶ Κύριε, δίδαξόν με τὰ δικαιώματά σου — Blessed art thou, O Lord; teach me thy statutes.'' The verse is chanted before each hymn, except for the last two in the series.

[179]There are Sundays when the Amomos is not read as a Kathisma and the Evlogetaria are not chanted. See *Τυπικὸν τῆς τοῦ Χριστοῦ Μεγάλης 'Εκκλησίας,''* Προθεωρία, 20, 21, 22, σελ. 19-20.

[180]In the weekly festal cycle Saturday is dedicated to the martyrs and the dead. This observance may be rooted in the Great Saturday event, i.e., Christ crucified (martyred), dead and lying in the tomb; conquering death by death.

[181]The funereal Evlogetaria would be totally inappropriate for Christ because of their content. Two of these hymns have the martyrs in mind; while the others in the series refer to men and women who lay claim to God's Kingdom and plead for God's mercy and salvation.

[182]This exceptionally beautiful and meaningful poem was authored by three different hymnographers. The original Canon comprised only four Odes, the present sixth, seventh, eighth and ninth, written by Cosmas the Melodist. Years later Kassiane completed the Canon by adding the hymns of the first, third, fourth and fifth Ode. In a further development Mark, a monk of the Sabbaite monastery and later Bishop of Idron, replaced the hymns which Kassiane wrote with his own, keeping only the eirmos (initial hymn) of the Odes written by her. See P. N. Trembelas, *'Εκλογὴ 'Ελληνικῆς 'Ορθοδόξου Ὑμνογραφίας* (Athens, 1949), p. 249.

[183]The initial procession of the Epitaphios at the Vespers of Great Friday is usually referred to as the ἔξοδος — exodus of the Epitaphios, because it is being "brought out" for veneration. This second procession is usually called the perifora (literally, to carry round) or procession of the Epitaphios.

[184]For brief descriptions of the order of the procession see e.g., *The Patriarchal Text of Great Week* (1906 edition), p. 278; the *Typikon*, p. 363; and the *Lenten Triodion*, p. 654. As Taft suggests, the procession of the Epitaphios probably originated in the Orthros of Great Saturday around the fourteenth century. It dramatized an earlier practice. In the Cathedral Office of Constantinople, the Scriptures were read at the conclusion of the Orthros after the Doxology. The readings were preceded by the procession of the Gospel. By the fourteenth century, on Great Saturday this procession had acquired a solemn mimetic character. The Gospel, as mentioned above, was wrapped in the aer and carried flat on the shoulder in imitation of Joseph of Arimathea carrying the body of Jesus to the tomb (Jn 19.17). This procession was further embellished with the introduction of the Epitaphios. Later, the Epitaphios was introduced to the Vespers of Great Friday as well. See, S. Janeras, *Le Vendredi-Saint* pp. 393-402; and R. Taft, ''In the Bridegroom's Absence,'' pp. 82-93 and especially p. 90.

[185]In large cities in Greece, e.g., and especially at Cathedral Churches, the procession is conducted in a grand manner. The procession is preceded by military guards and bands. The route is extended beyond the courtyards of the Church. Often the processions of several parishes converge at a central square.

[186]The rubric concerning the way the Gospel is held is an important detail. We have noted above that the Epitaphios developed around the thirteenth — fourteenth centuries. Before this period the Evangelion or Gospel served the same purpose. In the tradition of the Church, the Gospel is considered to be *the* icon of Christ. Thus, at the Vespers on Great Friday and the Orthros on Great Saturday, it was the Gospel itself, wrapped in the aer, that was carried in procession. The aer symbolized the burial cloth. To further accentuate the observance of the death of Christ, the priest held the Gospel flat upon his right shoulder. The Epitaphios has long since become the focus of attention. Nevertheless, the rubrics still require that the Gospel be carried by the priest in both processions. Also, significant is the fact that the Gospel is placed in the Kouvouklion upon the Epitaphios. This, too, is a carry over from the earlier practice before the develop-

ment of the Epitaphios. See Ioannis Fountoulis, Ἀπαντήσεις εἰς Λειτουργικὰς Ἀπορίας, Γ? (Thessalonike, 1976), pp. 18-22.

[187]Traditionally, the Cross and Epitaphios are carried by the clergy. However, in the absence of an adequate number of clergy, it has become the practice to allow lay persons to carry the Cross and the Epitaphios at this procession. These persons are designated in accordance with local customs.

[188]We have noted above that the procession of the Epitaphios on Great Friday and Saturday has its origins in the Great Entrance of the Divine Liturgy. Medieval texts describing the order of the Great Entrance indicate that the Epitaphios was carried last, preceded by deacons carrying the candles, hexapteryga and the Gifts. Frescoes depicting the heavenly liturgy also show the same order. See, Robert Taft, *The Great Entrance*, pp. 210-212.

[189]Besides the "῾Άγιος ὁ Θεός," the Patriarchal Text includes a lengthy hymn "Τόν ἥλιον κρύψαντα," as an additional processional hymn.

[190]In the Slavic tradition the Epitaphios is brought into the sanctuary at the Paschal Vigil, before the Orthros of the Resurrection. The placing the Epitaphios on the Holy Table symbolizes the entombment of Christ.

[191]Because of the joy of the Paschal season, it was considered inappropriate to process with the Epitaphios at the Great Entrance. Hence, the custom developed to keep it on the holy Table until the Apodosis of Pascha. We no longer carry the Epitaphios at the Great Entrance. Its use has been limited to Great Week. When the Epitaphios is removed at the feast of the Apodosis, it is stored or displayed in an appropriate place.

[192]This configuration of the Readings as well as their position in the order of the service is reminiscent of the Cathedral Office. In the Cathedral rite of Constantinople the Readings were placed at the end of the services of the daily office. The defunct Typikon of the Great Church also contains this same set of Readings for the Ortros of Great Saturday. See, Mateos, *Le Typicon*, vol. I, pp. xxii-xxiv; and vol. II, p. 82.

[193]See, The Patriarchal Text (1985), p. 320.

[194]In medieval times, at noon on Great Saturday the Patriarch and Emperor, accompanied by members of their respective courts, came to Hagia Sophia. Prior to their arrival the Church was incensed. The Emperor changed the cloth (ἡ ἐνδυτής) of the holy Table, after which the Patriarch incensed the altar and nave with the katzion. When these acts were accomplished, the doors of the Church were opened. See, Mateos, *Le Typicon*, p. 84; and G. Bertoniere, *Vigil*, pp. 121-24.

[195]See, Mateos, *Le Typicon*, pp. 78-82, "Τῇ ἁγίᾳ καὶ μεγάλῃ Παρασκευῇ . . . Ἑσπέρας δέ, μετὰ τὴν ἄνοιξιν τῆς ἐκκλησίας, ἡ προανάγνωσις καὶ τὰ τρία ἀντίφωνα, καὶ εἰς τὸ «Κύριε ἐκέκραξα» γίνεται εἴσοδος τοῦ Πατριάρχου μετὰ τοῦ μεγαλείου . . . Εἶτα λέγει ὁ διάκονος τὴν μεγάλην ἐκτενὴν καὶ τὰ λοιπὰ τῶν προηγιασμένων . . ."

[196]See John Karmiris, *A Synopsis of the Dogmatic Theology of the Orthodox Catholic Church*, (Scranton, 1973), pp. 55-74.

[197]Emmanuel Clapsis, "Life and Death in Eschatological Perspective," in Ἐκκλησία καί Θεολογία, vol. 5 (1984), p. 548.

[198]Raymond E. Brown, *The Gospel According to John* (Garden City, 1966) 1, cxvii.

[199]Georges Florovsky, "On the Tree of the Cross," *SVTQ* 1 3/4 (1953) 25.

[200]Ἔκδοσις Ἀκριβὴς Ὀρθοδόξου Πίστεως, 3,27, PG 94.1097.

[201]G. Florovsky, "On the Tree of the Cross," p. 16. St. John of Damascus suggests

that the word corruption can be thought of in two ways. First, the word refers to all the passive states of man, such as hunger, thirst, weariness, and death itself. In this sense the Lord's body was subject to corruption. The word, in its proper sense, has another meaning: the complete decomposition and destruction of the body. The Lord's body did not suffer this mode of corruption. Instead in death it was transfigured into a body of glorification.

[202]It is important to note that this truth has its application as well in Orthodox iconography. The dead body of Christ is never depicted as a corpse.

[203]*Deification In Christ* (Crestwood, 1987), p. 65.

[204]E. Clapsis, "Life and Death," p. 530.

[205]E. Clapsis, "Life and Death," p. 547.

[206]G. Florovsky, "The 'Immortality' of the Soul" in his collected works, vol. 3, *Creation and Redemption* (Belmont, 1976), p. 222.

[207]G. Florovsky, "On the Tree of the Cross," p. 20.

[208]G. Florovsky, "On the Tree of the Cross," p. 25.

[209]Περὶ τῆς 'Ενανθρωπήσεως τοῦ Λόγου, 21, PG 25.132.

[210]G. Florovsky, "On the Veneration of the Saints," in *Creation and Redemption*, p. 203.

[211]St. Symeon the New Theologian, Chapters, 3.88, in Basil Krivocheine, *In the Light of Christ* (Crestwood, 1986), p. 296.

[212]Catechetical Sermons 13:35-40, in B. Krivocheine, In the Light, p. 302.

[213]Ethics 7.598, in B. Krivocheine, *In the Light*, p. 294.

[214]See Emilianos Timiadis, *The Nicene Creed — Our Common Faith* (Philadelphia, 1983), p.63.

[215]Georgios Mantzaridis, *The Deification of Man* (Crestwood, 1984), p. 118.

[216]G. Florovsky, "On the Tree of the Cross," p. 25.

[217]G. Florovsky, "On the Tree of the Cross," p. 25.

[218]Ethics 10, in B. Krivocheine, *In the Light*, p. 308.

[219]Ethics 10, in B. Krivocheine, *In the Light*, p. 308.

[220]G. Florovsky, "The Last Things and the Last Events" in *Creation and Redemption*, p. 261. Theologians sometimes use the terms hell, hades and death interchangeably. One example of this is the following description of hell by Fr. Boris Bobrinskoy: "Hell is the place of infinite hopelessness and despair, the state of ultimate separation from God. It is a state we bear within ourselves even now in germinal form. Assuming the supreme solitude of His divine agony, Christ allows Himself to be dragged down into the winter night of death. There, in the realm of non-existence where lie the shadows of death and solitude, contact with His divinity communicates both life and light. The Orthodox Church has placed this conviction at the heart of its faith, its message, its liturgical life and prayer: by His passage through the realm of death, Christ has destroyed death; He has deprived it of its sting ... Within the framework of history, the gates of hell and the very reality of hell remain forever broken asunder." In, "Old Age and Death: Tragedy or Blessing" *SVTQ* 28/4 (1984) 241-42.

[221]G. Florovsky, "Redemption" in *Creation and Redemption*, p. 125. See also St. John of Damascus, ῎Εκδ. 'Ακρ. 4, 27; PG 94.1220-28.

[222]Dumitru Staniloae, *Theology and the Church* (Crestwood, 1980), p. 193.

[223]See Sergei Bulgakov, "Meditations on the Joy of the Resurrection," in A. Schmemann, *Ultimate Questions* (New York, 1965), pp. 299-309. Kallistos Ware, *The*

Orthodox Way (Crestwood, 1979), pp. 178-85. G. Florovsky, "Creation and Creaturehood" in *Creation and Redemption* pp. 43-78. John Meyendorff, *Byzantine Theology* pp. 129-37. John H. McKenna, "The Eucharist, the Resurrection and the Future," in *Anglican Theological Review* 60 (1978) 144-65.

[224]John Zizioulas, *Being As Communion* pp. 96, 98.

[225]D. Staniloae, *Theology and the Church* p. 206.

[226]At Constantinople the service of Baptism was conducted in the Great Baptistry, a distinct structure adjacent to the Church of Hagia Sophia.

[227]This volume has appeared in the series, *Orientalia Christiana Analecta*, 193 (Rome, 1972).

[228]See Bertoniere, *Easter Vigil*, pp. 157-61.

[229]The tenth hour is the equivalent of our 4 p.m. According to the Byzantine method of reckoning time, the day and night are divided equally into two twelve hour segments. One for the day and the other for the night. Thus, sunrise and sunset are at one and the same both the twelfth hour and the zero hour. Sunrise is both the twelfth hour of the night (its end) and the zero hour of the daytime (its beginning). Conversely, the sunset is the twelfth hour of the day and the zero hour of the nighttime. Each twelve hour segment is divided into four three hour intervals. The major intervals of the day are called Hours (First Hour, approximately our 6 a.m.; Third Hour, our 9 a.m.; Sixth Hour, our 12 noon; Ninth, our 3 p.m.). The same intervals mark the night time. The night intervals are usually called watches (First watch, our 6-9 p.m.; Midnight, our 9-12 midnight; Orthros, our 12-3 a.m.; Cockcrow, our 3-6 a.m.). The length of the two segments varies according to the season. Also, it must be noted that according to the Roman-Byzantine method, each new day begins at midnight or at the Sixth Hour of the night.

[230]See *Typikon of the Great Church of Christ*, pp. 364-73. Compare Ἀγία καὶ Μεγάλη Ἐβδομάς, 1906, pp. 284-320.

[231]The fact that the entire text of a hymn, together with the tone in which it is to be sung, is included in the narrative of the Typikon is an indication that it is a relatively new or a previously optional element which is now being given permanency.

[232]Semandra are wooden slabs of varying widths and lengths. They are struck with a mallet to produce sounds. Semandra can be carried or be suspended. A variety of sounds and beats are employed, appropriate to the occasion and service.

[233]*Typikon*, pp. 367-68.

[234]*Typikon*, p. 368.

[235]The Typikon of 1888 does not include the title Orthros. The entire service, beginning with the "Pannychis," is presented as a single untitled liturgical unit. I have inserted the titles for purposes of clarity.

[236]*Typikon*, p. 369.

[237]*Typikon*, p. 371.

[238]*Typikon*, p. 371.

[239]*Typikon*, p. 371.

[240]*Typikon*, p. 371.

[241]The custom of lighting candles in connection with the Jerusalem Paschal Vigil is quite old. It is mentioned in both the Armenian and Georgian Lectionaries.

[242]See Auxentios (Bishop) *The Holy Fire* (Etna, 1991). The author views the phenomenon as miraculous. He traces the history of the Holy Fire and provides the reader with accounts describing the event.

[243]Bertoniere, *Easter Vigil*, pp. 285-86.

[244]Bertoniere, *Easter Vigil,* p. 159.

[245]Bertoniere, *Easter Vigil,* p. 286. This act, however, should not be construed as a direct transference of the ceremony of the Holy Light, nor as a parallel to it.

[246]The time, however, at which the two ceremonies are conducted do not correspond. The Jerusalem ceremony of the Holy Light, once conducted within the context of the Paschal Vespers, is now celebrated on Great Saturday afternoon. Our present rite is really an embellished version of the simple ritual mentioned in the printed Typikon of 1545, and occurs before the Paschal Orthros.

[247]St. Germanos of Constantinople, e.g., gives the following meanings to the Holy Table: "The Holy Table corresponds to the spot in the Tomb where Christ was placed . . . The Holy Table is also the throne of God . . . The altar corresponds to the holy tomb of Christ. On it Christ brought Himself as a sacrifice to God the Father . . . through whom we have become sharers in eternal and immortal life." See Paul Meyendorff, *St. Germanus of Constantinople, On the Divine Liturgy* (Crestwood, 1984), pp. 58-61.

[248]*Typikon* pp. 367-68.

[249]N. Neokleous, *'Η 'Αγία καὶ Μεγάλη 'Εβδομάς,* p. 301. This ceremony was in force for more than a decade before the publication of this volume in 1906. It is mentioned in the text *'Ακολουθία Κατανυκτικὴ τῆς 'Αγίας καὶ Μεγάλης Τεσσαρακοστῆς,* compiled and published in Athens by Emmanuel Liodopoulos in 1895.

[250]This pericope is the second of the Eleven Morning Gospels read in rotation at the Sunday Orthros service.

[251]See, for example, the later editions of the Patriarchal Text, as well as E. Liodopoulos, *Μεγάλη Τεσσαρακοστή,* pp. 535-36; and the Greek-English Texts published by Williams and Norgate and George Papadeas.

[252]See I. Fountoules, *'Απαντήσεις εἰς Λειτουργικάς 'Απορίας* (Athens, 1967), pp. 168-71.

[253]I. Fountoules, *'Απαντήσεις* p. 169.

[254]I. Fountoules, *'Απαντήσεις* p. 169.

[255]Mk. 16.2, Mt. 28.1; Lk. 24.1; Jn. 20.1.

[256]The Church of Constantinople developed three Divine Liturgies: St. Basil, St. John Chrysostom and the Pre-Sanctified. In time these Liturgies became the common inheritance of all the Orthodox Churches. In the beginning, the Divine Liturgy of St. Basil was the established Liturgy of Constantinople. Its preeminent position lasted until the twelfth century, when it was supplanted by the Liturgy of St. John Chrysostom. The Liturgy of St. Basil was then gradually limited to ten celebrations in the course of the liturgical year, all of which coincide with the great festivals of the Church: the vigils of Pascha, Christmas and Epiphany; Great Thursday; and the five Sundays of Lent. It is also celebrated on the feast of St. Basil on January 1st. Earlier, it was also celebrated on Pentecost and on the feasts of the Annunciation and the Elevation of the Cross. Thus, the fact that the Liturgy of St. Basil is attached to the Paschal Vespers points to the significance of the Vesperal Liturgy in the scheme of the Paschal Vigil. See, A. Calivas, *Χρόνος Τελέσεως* pp. 144-53.

[257]The ceremony is mentioned by George Kodinos (ca. 15th century), in the work *Περὶ ὀφφικιαλίων τοῦ παλατίου Κωνσταντινουπόλεως καὶ τῶν ὀφφικίων τῆς Μεγάλης 'Εκκλησίας* edited and published by J. Verpeaux, *Traité des offices* (Paris, 1966), pp. 231-32.

[258]In many places, the floor is covered completely with leaves or some other sweet-smelling branches. The leaves remain in place throughout Renewal Week.

[259]This service is referred to as Pannychis in many of the newer liturgical texts. However, it should not be confused with the service of the Cathedral Office of the same name.

[260]An attempt in recent years to introduce yet another new element in the Pannychis has been gaining much ground. In many places, when the Canon has been completed, and the lights have been turned off and the lamps and candles have been extinguished, it has become a practice to sing the Seventh Morning Doxastikon of the Sunday Orthros, the hymn "'Ἰδοὺ σκοτία καὶ πρωΐ . . .'" This hymn does not appear in any official liturgical texts of the Paschal Vigil.

[261]The rubrics of the ancient monastic Typika indicate that the lamps were not lit during the Pannychis. It is noted that the ecclesiarch remained in the Church to light the lamps and the censers, when everyone else assembled in the Narthex after the Pannychis.

[262]This form of the opening doxology is characteristic of the monastic office. The form — Εὐλογημένη ἡ βασιλεία . . . — Blessed is the Kingdom . . ." is characteristic of the Cathedral Office. The simpler form "Εὐλογητὸς ὁ Θεός . . . — Blessed is our God . . ." used in many services represents an old venerable tradition.

[263]The Canon of Pascha was written by St. John of Damascus.

[264]In monasteries the doors of the nave are usually closed during the intermediate service. Before or after the Χριστὸς 'Ανέστη, according to local custom, the Royal Door is sealed three times with the sign of the cross and incensed. The doors are then opened and the Entrance is made. In some places a ceremony is conducted at the opening of the doors. This ceremony involves the use of Ps 23 (24) vv. 7-10 in dialogue form. The ritual, however, did not gain wide use nor did it receive the approbation of Church authorities. For this reason it did not find its way into the printed texts of Great Week and Pascha.

[265]Certain elements of the regular Sunday Orthros are absent from the Paschal Orthros. Among these are the Hexapsalmos, Kathismata, Anavathmoi, Gospel lesson, Psalm 50 (with its troparia and intercessary prayer-petition), and the Great Doxology. The priestly prayers, while omitted in current parish usuage, normally would precede the doxological endings of the Litanies.

[266]This longer list is found in the appendices of the book, p. 361. A translation of these twelve megalynaria may be found in the Greek-English text of Great Week published in London by Williams and Norgate in 1915. The megalynaria are interpolated verses and are called such because they begin (at least the first verse) with the word μεγαλύνω — magnify.

[267]Unfortunately, in many places this practice has fallen into disuse. Where possible it should be reinstated. According to the rubric noted in the 1888 Typikon of the Great Church, the priest holds the Gospel and the people file by to reverence the Gospel. This rubric does not mention the exchange of the kiss, which was by then limited to reverencing the Gospel, but earlier typika note the exchange. I am afraid that in most large parishes today it would be difficult and cumbersome to accomplish the rubric of the Typikon. Instead the priest may simply invite the faithful to exchange the kiss of peace, as it is done normally at the Divine Liturgy.

[268]The 1985 edition of the Patriarchal Text inserts the Paschal Homily attributed to St. John Chrysostom between the Orthros and the Divine Liturgy. However, the 1888 Typikon and the 1906 first edition of the Patriarchal Text and other subsequent editions place this homily in the Divine Liturgy after Holy Communion. I suspect that the editor has placed the homily at the end of the Orthros because many people leave the service early. The editor suggests that the homily could be read after the Gospel in the place of a sermon. The paschal and eucharistic themes in the homily certainly commend it as a sermon, which should be heard before and not after Holy Communion. It is my opinion that it should be read after the Gospel.

[269]Most liturgical books place the homily of St. John Chrysostom at this point. However, as we noted above, the homily should be read before holy Communion because of the eucharistic themes it contains.

[270]*Typikon*, p. 372.

[271]The order as set forth in these texts is clear. Slight variations, however, may occur, when for example, the feast of St. George is celebrated on Monday of Renewal Week. The hymns of the saint are added to the Paschal troparia in accordance with the rubrics in the Typikon.

[272]For a description of the order of this prelimanary service, see the *Typikon*, p. 372.

[273]The first edition of the Patriarchal Text contained the text of the Gospel in several languages, in the original and in Greek phonetics. Subsequent editions duplicated these texts. Of special interest is the fact that the more recent editions of the Patriarchal Text have added other languages and especially the languages of the "diaspora" and Mission Churches. The 1985 edition, e.g., contains the following languages (in the order appearing in the text): Ancient Greek (in Hexameter), Slavonic, Serbian, Romanian, Albanian, Arabic, Turkish, Armenian, Latin, Italian, French, German, English, Korean, and Swahili.

[274]The same order is followed throughout Renewal Week. The Introductory Psalm 103 (Προοιμιαχός) is not read. After Renewal Week, the Χριστὸς ᾿Ανέστη is chanted only three times at the beginning of every service, after the opening doxology.

[275]In some places it has become the practice to exchange the kiss of peace at this service during the singing of this hymn.

CPSIA information can be obtained at www.ICGtesting.com
Printed in the USA
BVOW040247281211

279183BV00002B/5/A